Hanratty - The Final Curtain

David J Cooper

Published by David J Cooper, 2021.

HANRATTY - THE FINAL CURTAIN

First edition. December 23, 2021.

Written by David J Cooper.

Table of Contents

Dedicated to Tony Holdcroft, a lifetime friend

INTRODUCTION

Sixty years ago a small time thief, James Hanratty, with no history of violent crime was hanged for a motiveless and horrific murder, but vital evidence, withheld from the original trial, indicated that he might have been wrongly executed.

His defence counsel couldn't take it in that this evidence had been concealed.

At the same time, new DNA discoveries by forensic scientists told a very different story.

If the interpretation of the DNA was right then James Hanratty was guilty, but if other new evidence, kept secret from the trial was right, then he might be innocent.

What is the truth in this case?

Was he innocent or guilty?

Is this DNA evidence a cover up for the British government?

Is this the final curtain on the James Hanratty case?

What is your opinion after reading this book?

CHAPTER ONE

H is eyes were drawn away as a woman with platinum blonde hair and a tight mini skirt sauntered up to the bar, eyeing the regulars like an aging lioness hungry for a meal.

After a slight hesitation, he took a deep breath and started.

"Val.....I know this isn't what you want to hear but Janet won't give me a divorce," he said.

There was no heat in her voice as she looked at him through her horn rimmed glasses and simply said, "That comes as no surprise."

When the tension in him went, when the relief began, he carried on as normal, only somewhat happier than before.

"What do you think?" he asked. "Do you want us to carry on as we are or shall we call it a day?"

"If all I am to you is a bit on the side then I love you for always and forever but I know you don't think of me in that way. Our good times outnumber the bad by multitudes and I accept that Janet won't give you a divorce. Mind you, I can't blame her," she replied.

"So you want to continue our relationship?" he asked.

"I want it to go on forever," she replied.

Her smile was one of happiness growing, much like a spring flower opening. It came from deep inside to light her eyes and spread into every part of her.

Michael could feel her smile. He heard it in her voice, in her choice of words and the way she was so relaxed.

The Old Station Inn at Taplow was the very epitome of what a good village community pub should be. It was well maintained, inviting and humble. Wooden beams supported the upper floor and the chandeliers attached to them. The walls were decorated with sports memorabilia, indicating that the owners, and probably the customers, were avid fans.

The few people inside could be anybody, but whoever they were, they were enjoying each other's company.

What stood out like a sore thumb was the man sitting silently opposite them. He made her a little nervous. He looked like a drifter and his gaze was riveted to her. His short, greased, dark hair slightly revealed a full, tense face. There was something about him which made her feel uneasy.

"Mike," she said, kicking his leg underneath the table and carefully nodding her head in the man's direction. "Do you know that man sitting opposite?"

He glanced up.

"No," he replied. "Why?"

"He's giving us some funny looks," she replied.

"Shall I go and ask him what he's looking at?" he asked.

"No," she replied. "We don't want any trouble in here. Let's drink what's left of our beers and leave. We can discuss the motor rally another day."

They had been doing their best, over a couple of pints of beer, to work out a system of penalty marks for the ambitious all day rally they were trying to organize through the Chiltern Hills.

The half a dozen or so people that had been in the bar had now become around two dozen. It was a quarter to nine.

They tipped back their drinks and left.

Valerie Storie met Michael Gregsten at the Road Research Laboratory at Langley, near Slough, Buckinghamshire, where they were doing research work. They actually met at the Canteen Committee,

2

which she had joined. Their first date was at a dance just before Christmas. He asked her in a friendly, jocular way, if she would be his partner at the dance.

She knew he was married, but he had told her that his wife didn't like dancing.

She was nineteen at the time and knew that he was fourteen years older than her.

It was love at first sight for her as she fell for his boyish looks and his softly spoken voice.

She, on the other hand, was quite a plain Jane.

He and his wife had separated when she learned of his affair with Valerie. They had two children, both boys.

All there was at first was a friendship between them.

Michael was important to her because he made her feel necessary and important. She considered him only as Michael - not as Michael the married man and father of two children.

He was a good conversationalist. No matter what the subject, he always had a ready answer. They used to discuss all sorts of topics.

They shared a liking for cars, serious music, concerts and theatre going. She knew that Michael was attracted towards her. She was young and was excited. She had never felt like this before and looked forward to seeing him again. Soon there were regular phone calls. He began to help her with her maths, for she was studying at night school for her Advanced G.C.E. in maths. Sometimes they would fix a date. She liked this sense of belonging - that there was someone at last in her life for which she was a special sort of person. All this time her affection for Michael was a very private thing. She never thought that having an affair with a married man was wrong – at the time. She used to say to herself, "But if I am sincere, if I really and truly am fond of Michael, how can it be wrong?"

They had met. They liked to talk together. Other things happened. For a long time things went on like this. She kept her secret to herself.

They never really worked out how things were going to end up. Every time they got around to talking about things like that they could never arrive at any sort of decision.

The children were an ever present concern in his mind.

Her parents had met Mike - indeed they had welcomed him into their home but they didn't know he was a married man. She hated keeping this from them, but felt they wouldn't understand.

Finally her secret leaked out in the worst way. Someone tittle tattled to her mother. When she asked her if it was true and she said yes, her parents didn't interfere. She told her mother not to worry assuring her that nothing would happen to her. Her parents knew her well enough to realize that she couldn't be forced to forget about Michael. She was the sort of person who could be led but never forced. So the open door stayed open at their house for him. Their love began to grow richer.

Michael and Valerie were both very keen on motor rallying and had gone to the pub to discuss plans on a forthcoming rally.

Although it was the swinging sixties, people still frowned on young women having affairs with married men and it was this that worried her. She thought the man might have known Michael's wife and was some sort of private detective observing them.

The evening sun cast long shadows on the car park as they left the pub and headed towards the grey Morris Minor he had borrowed from his aunt. Like the gentleman he was, Michael opened the front passenger door for Valerie and she stepped in.

"Do you want to go back to my place?" he asked, as he put the key into the ignition.

"No," she replied. "It's a nice evening. Let's go to our special place near the river."

The engine started and he slowly made his way out of the car park.

It wasn't long before there were fields all around them, their patterns only broken by the occasional tree left to grow in peace.

Cows and sheep were grazing in the fading light of the late August evening.

They eventually arrived at an opening in a nearby cornfield at Dorney Reach where a flock of cows had found something newsworthy.

Michael pulled the car off the country lane and drove a few yards into the field which was used by lovers.

Usually there were other cars dotted around but that evening they had the place to themselves.

The sweet, slightly pungent smell of the corn moved in steady waves as they sat inside the snugness of the car, watching the sunset sink perfectly into the field in a balance of pink and gold. The occasional barking of dogs in the distance broke the silence.

She didn't need a drink or food – just the pure pleasure of nuzzling up close – with her man's arm around her while the sunset matched their breathing.

They were parked with their backs to the roadway. Occasionally a tug of wind bustled against the windows and the car gave a little tremble.

They had been quite a few times in the car to that particular spot.

In the summer they had parked up and wandered down to the river to watch the boats go by through the locks. They always enjoyed their evenings by the river. That particular night had started happily enough. Mike had gone to her house for tea and afterwards they drove to the pub.

They sat there in the car finalizing the plans for the next motor rally which was a rather ambitious eighty mile route.

She felt very close to him.

It was the 22nd August 1961 and the dusk had faded in so slowly that they failed to notice until the field ahead of them was disappearing into darkness.

An unexpected tapping at the window had her frozen. It was no more than a tap but in the failing light her heart was on a hair-trigger. From the moment that tap came at the window life stopped for both of them.

CHAPTER TWO

It took a second or two for Valerie to realize what was happening. She looked at Michael clutching the steering wheel, his hands wrapped so tightly around it that his nails dug into his palm. The blood pounded in her ears. Her heart thudded in her chest. Her hands shook. Her feet tingled. Her vision disfigured, as if she were looking through a fish eye lens.

Who was this interrupting their magic world?

At first she thought a farmer wanting to get his harvesting machine through the gateway had found them.

But this was no farmer or farmer's lad. The figure standing perfectly still looked like a shop window dummy. He was immaculately dressed in a clean and crisp dark suit, white shirt and tie.

Her chest grew tight as bile rose in her throat. But this time there was something of fear in her reaction. The man's face was half covered with a handkerchief. He looked sinister silhouetted there against the rapidly darkening August sky.

Mike began to wind down the window, and then without warning the man thrust a gun into the car.

Many thoughts ran through Valerie's mind in that split second. Relief that it must be a joke, fear in case what was happening was real.

Surely it must be a game, a man playing at gangsters to see what their reaction would be?

Yes, that was it. She felt so certain about this that she turned to Michael and almost began to giggle. Surely this was a toy pistol?

The figure of a man was on Michael's side of the car. She looked from this shadowy outline to Michael then stopped. She could sense that he was worried – almost frightened,

He rolled down the window and the man said, "This is a hold up. I'm a desperate man. I've been on the run for four months so don't do anything silly."

"Give me the keys," he said, waving the gun at Michael.

Opening the rear door he eased his way into the back seat.

This sort of thing doesn't happen to ordinary people. It happens in films and on television.

It seemed so farcical, so utterly ridiculous.

She remembered thinking what an adventure this would be. In a flash she could see Mike and her talking about the whole mad cycle later on.

Then things began to grow real. The man wanted money and food.

"I'm hungry," he said. "I haven't eaten for two days and I've been sleeping rough the last two nights. Have you got any chocolate?"

Valerie couldn't believe him because of his appearance. She dipped into her handbag and felt her hand close over her wallet. She'd been to the bank that day and no way was this man going to have her money.

She wrapped her fist round the notes and quickly tucked them away inside her bra. She told herself that he would never dare look there and felt rather cunning and clever that she had managed to fool him.

"I don't have any chocolate," she said. "Who are you? What do you want?"

"Be quiet will you? I'm finking," he replied. "Anyway, what are you two doing out here in this field? Done some bonking, have we?"

"We were planning a motor rally," replied Mike.

"Do you think I'm falling for that?" he asked. "You've just been inside her knickers. I've been watching you. I saw the car wobble from side to side more than once." He looked at Val and said, "Fancy a bit with a complete stranger?"

"Leave her alone," said Mike.

"Are you married?" he asked.

"No we aren't," replied Val.

"Don't look so worried," he said. "You will be all right if you do as I tell you."

"What's your name?" he asked, glaring at Michael

"Michael," he replied.

"And yours?" he asked, nodding to Valerie.

"Valerie," she replied. "What's your name?"

"You can call me Jim," he replied. "I've been in the Oxford area for the last few days," he continued. "I never had a chance in life. When I was a child I used to get locked in the cellar for days on end and only had bread to eat and water to drink. I have been in and out of remand homes and Borstal. In fact, I've done the lot. I did five years for house breaking and now every policeman in England is looking for me."

During the course of the incident, the man took their watches.

For two long hours they all sat there then unexpectedly he pointed the gun at Mike's head.

It was now around 11.30 pm.

"Move this thing out of here," he said. "Drive us to the nearest café. I'm thirsty."

Mike turned the key in the ignition, took a long, slow, deep breath and as he edged the car out of the field the man took over as navigator.

Mike was driving calmly enough but from time to time she looked in the rear view mirror and saw a tight, worried look in his eyes.

They did exactly as the man instructed and no more.

"Do you know what?" he said. "I've never shot anybody before. This gun is like a cowboy pistol. I feel like a cowboy pulling off a stunt."

"What do you want?" asked Michael.

"There's no hurry," he replied, raising his voice.

He tapped his pocket and they heard the rattle of bullets.

She touched Mike's hand. He took his left hand off the steering wheel and ran his fingers over hers.

"Concentrate on your driving," the man said, giving the gun a jerk.

Mike concentrated on his driving again but as he raised his left hand back on the steering wheel, he flicked the reversing light switch on without the man noticing what he'd done.

A passing car flashed at them as it went past no doubt trying to draw attention to it. But the hijacker spotted the interest the other car took in them.

"Stop the car," he ordered. "Get out and take me to the back of the car."

"What do you want to go to the back of the car for?" Mike asked.

"I want to inspect the rear lights," he replied.

"There's nothing wrong with the lights," Mike said.

"There's something wrong," the man said. "Why would that car flash his lights at you if there was nothing wrong?"

The man led him round to the back at gunpoint to inspect the rear lights.

Now Val had a big chance to escape. She was in the car. She was a good driver and could have easily slipped into the driver's seat and made a break for it.

Maybe the man would have fired the gun but he would have to be a good shot to kill a driver who was speeding away. She sensed that if she had done that the man would certainly kill Mike.

Up to now he had promised no harm would come to them if they did exactly as he told them.

He ordered Michael out of the car and to the vehicles boot, placing a blanket down so his hostage would be comfortable.

"Get in," he said.

"There's a leak in the exhaust that lets fumes come into the boot," Michael explained. "If I'm confined to this small space for a period of time I will surely die."

"You have a point," the hijacker said. "It's not a very good idea. Let's get back in the car."

They got back in the car.

"Now drive towards London," he said.

They'd been driving for about an hour when the man spotted something.

"Pull over at that milk machine," he said.

Unfortunately, nobody had a sixpenny piece to make a purchase so they continued on what should have been a twenty eight mile journey. They had been driving all over the English countryside when the fuel warning light came on and Michael pulled the car into a filling station near Heathrow airport.

He approached the pump attendant.

"Can you put two gallons in please?" he asked, trying to alert the attendant to what was happening in the car but failed to do so.

"That'll be nine shillings and nine pence," said the attendant.

Michel gave him a ten shilling note.

They drove on and the man gave directions. At one point in the Harrow area the man said, "Be careful. Round the corner there are some roadworks."

There was no sign to give any warning yet the man insisted he didn't know the area.

It was now just after midnight and he trio drove on to Stanmore.

Michael spotted a cigarette machine.

"Can I stop and get some cigarettes," he asked.

"Make it quick and don't try anything stupid," the man replied. "I don't smoke and I don't like smoking."

Mike had to walk across the road to get to the machine and could have made a run for it but he got the cigarettes and returned to the car so that Valerie wasn't left alone with the man.

The traffic had thinned considerably by the time the three drove north to St. Alban's and further north towards Luton. The Morris minor then joined the A6 heading towards Bedford, approximately sixty miles north of London. By this time, the man's eyes were getting heavy and he was constantly yawning. It was nearing one thirty in the morning.

"I need a kip," he said, looking out of the rear window for somewhere suitable to stop. He ordered Michael to pull over twice so he could have a sleep. But at times he changed his mind as they continued past the small village of Clophill. They continued up a hill when the man saw the perfect place to stop.

"Pull in over there in that layby," he said.

Mike had been taking orders from this man for over four hours and was getting a bit pissed off. But what could he do? So far no harm had come to him or Valerie as the man had promised but how much more could they take? Maybe once the man was asleep they could leave him in the middle of nowhere, drive away and escape. He pulled the car off the main highway and into the layby. The name of the area printed on a sign: *Dead Man's Hill.*

"I will have to tie you both up while I have a kip," he said. Waving the gun at Mike he said, "Get out of the car and come with me."

He searched the boot for something suitable to tie them up but couldn't find anything so they returned to the car. He took Michael's tie and tied Valerie's hands together with it.

"Please don't kill us," Valerie pleaded.

"If I was going to shoot you, I would have done it before now," he said. Looking at Michael he said, "Now I've got to find something to tie you up with."

"Why don't you use your tie?" Michael asked.

"No, I need that," he replied

The man then noticed a duffel bag of laundry near Valerie's feet and looking at Michael he said, "Pass that bag over."

Michael picked up the bag with both hands, turned towards the back of the car and as the bag was just about to go over the back of the seat when 'Crack, crack' the man shot him twice.

The bullets punched their way through his left cheek and ear, causing gaping holes in their wake which quickly filled with blood and gushed out. Michael slumped backwards, a pool of blood forming round him and soaking into his clothes.

He died instantly.

Valerie screamed, "You shot him, you bastard. Why? Why?"

"He frightened me. He moved too quickly and I got frightened," he replied.

She sat there sobbing.

"Be quiet will you?" he said. I'm trying to fink."

Once that first tear broke free, the rest followed in an unbroken stream. She bent forward where she was sitting and pressing her palms to the dashboard, she began to cry with the force of a person vomiting.

"Please let me get him to a doctor," she sobbed. "Leave us with a doctor and take the car and go."

They argued for nearly twenty minutes as to whether Michael should receive medical attention.

The man removed the handkerchief from his face.

"Kiss me," he said.

"Fuck you," she shouted.

"I'll count to five," he said, pointing the gun at her.

As she faced him another car came along, lighting up his face by the passing headlights and she got her first real glimpse of him. Those icy blue, staring eyes.

Would she ever forget them?

"Get into the back seat," he said, threatening her with the gun.

He was wearing black gloves and seemed to have difficulty getting them off and made her pull one of them off. She could feel that they were of a very thin nylon type texture.

Michael's was lying with his head over the steering wheel with blood gushing out.

The man covered Michael's face with a rag before raping her. While he was raping her, a few cars went past, but none for long enough that she could get another good to look at his face.

When he was finished, she said, "Take the car and go away."

"I'm in no hurry," he said. "We need to get rid of his body. Come on; give me a hand with it."

She dragged the body out of the driving seat and laid it down by the roadside.

Mike's hand was cold, stone cold and lifeless. She sat beside him. She didn't weep; she just sat there waiting for the murderer to go.

"Get up and come and show me how to start the car and use the gears," he said.

She went to the car and showed him.

He moved her out of the way, got into the car and stalled it twice.

She started the car for him again.

He hopped out of the driver's seat and left the engine running.

It was three thirty in the morning.

He went up to her and said, "I ought to hit you over the head with something and knock you out or you'll go for help."

"Here's a pound note," she said, taking it from her raincoat. "Just leave me and go."

He turned away and walked back towards the car.

When he was about six feet away from her, he turned around.

There was a crash and a bang and something hit her. She fell to her knees and then to the ground coming to rest next to Michael's body.

The man reloaded the gun.

HANRATTY - THE FINAL CURTAIN

There was another shot and another. She couldn't feel her legs. There was a click and more shots whined over her head.

She lay there not daring to breathe.

He went up to her, kicked her and walked away.

He calmly took the driver's side of the Morris Minor and with gears crunching, sped off towards London.

CHAPTER THREE

A metallic, sort of like licking a copper pot, but warm and deep sensation was in her mouth as she lay on the ground beside Michael.

"Why can't I feel my legs," she thought. "Am I going to die?"

The path beneath her faded as it led into the darkness, like a place out of time, yet she had to drag herself towards the gravel at the side of the road.

"I have to make a message with the rocks before I die," she said to herself.

But her hands were like those that could only lift a spoon and moving a small piece of gravel was like lifting weights for her.

All she could do was lie there hoping that in a short time the sun would kiss the sky orange and ignite a new dawn, bringing the chorus of birds and help.

As she lay there, her life with Michael was passing before her eyes.

He was important to her because he made her feel necessary and important. She considered him only as Michael - not as Michael the married man and father of two children.

His very difference attracted her. For instance, he loved continental food and Indian curry. She didn't know very much about that sort of thing. He was a good conversationalist. No matter what the subject, he always had a ready answer. They used to discuss all sorts of topics.

She went to cooking classes, though she didn't learn anything at all about continental food.

They shared a liking for cars, serious music, concerts and theatre going. In the beginning they were just good friends who never found any difficulty in telling each other what they thought and felt about anything.

But he was the emotional one. He had a temper, and she could see that it was her fear of throwing him into a tantrum which made her take a tough and practical line whenever he tried to unload his worries onto their relationship.

Sometimes bitter words would be spoken; but they valued their relationship, they didn't really want to quarrel and always made it up.

They were partners at a dance. Afterwards he took her home in his car.

They stopped at the end of her road, and she remembered how she felt as they sat in the car and he kissed her goodnight that this was the beginning of something exciting. All sorts of things suddenly seemed possible. She didn't seem a plain Jane any more.

She knew that Michael was attracted towards her. She was nineteen and excited. She had never felt like this before and looked forward to seeing him next time. Soon there were regular phone calls. He began to help her with her maths, for she was studying at night school for her Advanced G.C.E. in maths.

Sometimes they would fix a date. She liked this sense of belonging - that there was someone at last in her life to whom she was a special sort of person. He was beginning to be important.

All this time her affection for Michael was a very private thing.

She knew other people would say they were wrong. But anyone who has ever had an affair like this would agree with her that it never does seem wrong - at the time. She used to say to herself, "But if I am sincere, if I really and truly am fond of Michael, how can it be wrong?"

She knew that for both of them there was nothing nasty in their relationship.

They had met. They liked to talk together. Other things happened.

To her this was love, and she was sure it was like that with Michael.

How many people who have since criticized her have done so from the bitterness produced by their own unhappy marriages?

For a long time things went on like this. When other girls showed her their engagement rings and talked about their boyfriends, she kept her secret to herself. She could smile. For deep down within her she knew that she, too, possessed the love of a man - Michael.

Of course, Mike's wife knew about his friendship with her. She didn't know if she realized how far their friendship went.

Mike certainly adored his children. But he felt he needed her companionship. Somehow they fitted.

They never really worked out how things were going to end up. Every time they got around to talking about things like that they could never arrive at any sort of decision.

The children were an ever present concern in his mind. And she, too, had one guilty feeling which worried her at times.

They joined the office motor rally club. They loved the sense of freedom these rallies gave them.

Altogether they must have competed in about twenty of them - but they liked the all night ones best, they taxed their brains more.

They left home at about ten o' clock at night. Then out into the darkness, driving along in their private world together. Then the dawn.

They loved to watch the dawn break. That was always the time they felt least tired. At the end of the rally there was always bacon and egg breakfast and that happy, relaxed feeling that existed when a rally was over.

They never won anything more than a novice award, but they did have some marvellous times.

In the winter months when there were no car rallies they joined the works amateur dramatic society.

She remembered the part she got in a play called My Three Angels.

Mike used to tease her about it and say she'd end up in the West End. But this was only fun. Really they valued the dramatic society because it enabled them to do things together and to forget that in other ways they had so many difficulties in their life together.

By now Mike discussed marriage pretty freely. He told her he wanted to marry her if ever he became free to do so.

She wasn't unduly worried. She was happy. She preferred to take life as it happened. She lived every day as it came. It was no use brooding about things that might never happen.

Mike and she had been asked to help plan a car rally for the motor club at work. They were talking about this when they drove into that deserted field last night when everything exploded.

It began so ordinarily. Not a night for the wild, the unexpected, the terrible. Certainly not a night for any sort of anguish.

They sat in their car and were finalizing plans for the next motor rally, a rather ambitious eighty mile route.

And then, so unexpected and so alien that she remembered starting with surprise, the tap at the window.

From the moment that tap came at the window life stopped for both of them. But even then, not suddenly. Not dramatically. But in a long drawn anguish which was to be so horrible that within six short hour's horror itself became another word.

The rising sun cast a rosy hue across the morning sky as eighteen year old John Kerr was making his way to the RAC box near Deadman's Hill. He had a summer job with the Ministry of transport, counting the number of cars that passed by that location.

As he was walking along the overgrown country lane, golden fingers of sunlight were now lighting the area up. He stopped to smell the flowers; he admired the blue sky and smiled at the rabbits running across the meadow.

When he crossed the grassy knoll leading to the main road he saw something. At first he could have sworn it was a collection of something lying at the end of the road about eighty metres in front of him. But when he got nearer he felt a rush of fear wash over him. There were two bodies.

He realised that one of them was a woman lying on her back and beyond her another figure also on its back. He saw that the figure was wearing trousers so he assumed it must be a man.

Shivering feverishly, he moved closer to the woman. A slight and startling tingle tiptoed down his spine. He saw that her skirt was above her knees and her face and clothes were spattered in blood.

"Are you alright?" he asked.

"No," she replied. "I've been shot."

"What's your name?" he asked, jotting everything down on the back of one of the documents he was using to count the traffic with.

"Valerie Storie," she replied. "Please tell my parents. They'll be so worried about me. Stop the next car that comes along and tell them to get the police here."

It wasn't long before he heard the sound of a vehicle and flagged it down and told them to get the police and an ambulance then he returned to Valerie.

"Well what has happened," he asked.

"We picked up a man around nine thirty last night near Slough," she replied. "He drove us here."

The rampant pounding of John's heart accelerated as he looked at what appeared to be a piece of blue flannel covering Michael's face.

"Is he dead?" he asked.

"I think so," she replied.

"What was the man like?" he asked, still scribbling all of this down.

21

"He had big staring eyes, fairish brown hair, slightly taller than I am, and I am five foot three and a half inches," she replied. "When he left us he took our car which is number 847 BHN."

John could see that Valerie was shivering and wondered how long she'd been lying there. It was remarkable that hypothermia hadn't set in.

He struggled out of his coat and placed it around her. He noticed two empty cartridge cases nearby. He moved over to Michael and picked up his hand trying to feel for a pulse. It fell back with gravity, smack – unresponsive.

It didn't seem long before the police arrived on the scene.

"Was it you who found these people?" Inspector Edward Milborrow asked John.

"Yes," John replied. "Here are the notes I've taken down from what the young lady told me."

"Would you mind getting in that police car over there?" the Inspector asked. "We need to ask you more questions at the police station."

"No problem," John replied and got into the police car.

The ambulance came with aggressive speed, the kind of sheer driving audacity which let everyone know the siren wasn't a polite request to move. There was something in the intensity of the moment because the way it was being driven gave some emotional urgency. It was a welcome sight for Valerie.

She was placed in the rear of the ambulance and within an hour of her being found she was being treated in Bedford hospital.

CHAPTER FOUR

The clock on the King George Hospital, Ilford, was showing a few minutes after seven in the morning as John Skillett and his passenger Edward Blackhall, drove past on their way to work.

He was driving in the outside lane of the dual carriageway. The traffic lights were on red as he got nearer so he slowed down and left a gap between his car and the one in front.

As he was slowing down, a grey Morris Minor cut in from the inside lane and skidded to a halt, narrowly missing his car and the one in front.

"Where the fuck did he come from?" John said, pressing his lips and shaking his head.

The lights changed to green and the Morris Minor swerved into the nearside lane. The sound of its tyres skidding on the road shattered the immense silence that had been as it sped off.

John chased after him. As they were approaching a traffic roundabout, the Morris Minor was blocked by waiting traffic.

He managed to pull alongside it in the outside lane.

"Roll the window down, Ted," he said.

"Are you fucking mad or something?" he shouted. "You ought to get off the fucking road."

Edward simply shouted, "Get off the road."

The driver glared back at them curling his lip and turning up his nose. He let out a scornful laugh and sped away in the direction of

Redbridge Station. Without any indication, the car made a sharp turn right and disappeared from view.

Just around the corner, James Trower was standing on the pavement between Avondale Crescent and Redbridge Station. He'd just parked his car on the main road and had got out and was waiting to pick his workmate up. As he stood there he heard the sound of a car. He could hear a crunching noise that sounded as if the driver was trying to change gear. He turned around and saw a grey Morris Minor travelling slowly as it approached the junction in the road.

He saw that the driver was wearing a dark jacket and white shirt. The car turned into Avondale Crescent and disappeared from view. As he couldn't hear the engine anymore he assumed it had stopped.

After stopping the car, the suspect got out and went into Redbridge station. At six o' clock that evening, Detective Acott received the first break in the case; a man walking his dog on Avondale Crescent spotted the Morris Minor parked on the straight at an odd angle. The front number plate had been bent back and there was a dent in the rear bumper. There was blood spattered inside and outside of the car. A local resident reported the car having been parked there since seven forty five in the morning. There were no forensic fibres, hair or fingerprints present throughout the vehicle. However, two empty 38 calibre cartridge cases were found inside which matched similar ones found at the scene of the crime.

Later that evening, Edwin Cook, a cleaner for London Transport, was doing his job inspecting the buses at the garage in Peckham, South London.

He moved like someone schooled in dance. He wasn't cleaning so much as meditating, side stepping and turning in fluid motions as if the brush were a beloved partner as he moved it along the floor of the upper deck of the 36A bus. He reached the top of the stairs at the rear and leaned the brush against the rail leading down to the lower deck.

As he searched for rubbish, he lifted the back seat. He made a habit of checking this seat on every bus he claimed after once coming across two dead rats nestled in the space. On this occasion, he lifted up the seat. Stumbling back, his hands clutching the front of his shirt.

"What is that?" he gasped, narrowing his eyes as he stared at the handkerchief.

"Some dirty bastard has had the nerve to leave this snotty thing here."

He breathed in, held the air and let it out before finally picking it up between his finger and thumb.

Then a cold, tingling kind of numbness spread across his forehead, into his mouth, into his cheeks. He couldn't speak because the muscles in his mouth were paralysed. Even if he could speak, he wouldn't know what to say. His backside found the seat opposite, but he didn't remember sitting down. He was on auto pilot. He got his mouth to work again.

"What..." he was surprised by the hoarseness of his own voice. "The fuck have I found here?"

Staring him in the face was a fully loaded revolver and five boxes of ammunition.

The gun was quickly confirmed to be the 38 calibre used in the murder. The cleaner was positive the weapon and accessories had been deposited there that day as he had cleaned the same bus the night before.

The busy 36A bus travelled two routes that day throughout London. Police offered an amnesty for anyone who saw anything suspicious on the bus to come forward. Nobody did.

As detectives continued to hunt for the A6 gunman, both the families of Michael Gregsten and Valerie Storie were coming to terms with the attack that had forever changed their lives.

Michael's wife Janet was bereft at the loss of her husband and in an attempt to take her mind off things on August 31; she went to her brother-in-law William's shop in North London.

She was helping him set up a display in the storefront window when she noticed a man walking by. She grabbed William's arm and pointed to the man. He was slim, approximately five foot six inches and immaculately dressed in a suit. He had dark hair, a pale complexion and deep set eyes.

"Look at him, Bill," she said. "I don't know why but I have a gut feeling that he's the one who murdered Mike."

"What makes you say that?" William asked.

"I don't know," she replied. "But I've got this strong feeling that it's him. I can't explain. It's like my sixth sense is telling me. And his face resembles the identikit pictures that have been in the newspapers."

She was certain this was the man who had killed her husband as his face resembled identical images based on witness accounts of the man seen driving Michael's Morris minor in the hours following the shooting.

They watched him walk into a dry cleaner across the road.

"Go after him Bill," she snapped. "Go and give him a good hiding. You're a lot bigger than him."

"I can't just go and attack a complete stranger," he said, stepping back.

"Mike was your brother," she said. "That bastard murdered your brother in cold blood and all you can say is you can't attack a stranger. What are you a man or a mouse?"

"I understand what you're saying," he replied. "But you need to calm down. We have no proof whatsoever that he is the man who murdered Mike. Now leave it to me and I'll go and investigate once he's left."

A short while later William went to the dry cleaner.

"Good morning," he said to the lady behind the counter. "My sister in law and I noticed the man who has just left and was wondering if you could tell me who he is? She thinks she knows him but wants to be sure."

"Oh, he brought a green suit in to have tailored last week," she replied. "Let me have a look at the ticket. Hold on. It's a Mr J. Ryan."

"Thank you very much," he said.

"He lives in St. John's Wood," she said. "Would you like the address?"

"No, that's fine thanks," he replied. "If my sister in law knows him I'm sure she knows where he lives."

William now had something to work with.

He did not have to wait long before he ran into the man again.

The next day William was sitting at a café next to a florist on Finchley road in London.

He was lost in the mesmerizing aroma of the cup of tea he had in his hands. The delicious nectar gave him a beautiful experience of calmness and respite when a pair of exquisitely made leather shoes caught his eye.

As he looked up to see who was sporting them, he realized it was the same man he had seen from his shop the day before. The man went into the florist next to the café.

On any other day he would have smiled at people filling the café. He would have seen his future reflected in them. But not today. Waiting was easy for him. He'd had all the practice in his fishing days. For some people a day is a long time, a week even more. His concept of time was so different, he sat, let his mind empty and enjoyed the peace and soon his waiting for the man to leave the florist would be over.

When the man came out, William went in.

"I hope you don't mind," he said to young girl. "But could you tell me who that man is, the one who just walked out of the shop?"

"That's none of your business," she replied.

"But I think it is," he said. "That man is wanted for murdering my brother and I demand that you phone Scotland Yard."

"Is this a joke?" she asked.

"Does it look as though I'm joking?" he replied. "What did he want?" "He came in to send some rose to his mother," she replied. "They are being sent to Mrs Hanratty from J.Ryan."

"Don't you think it strange that his mother is named Hanratty and he's named Ryan?" he asked.

"What's strange about that?" she replied.

"He's supposed to be her son and has a different surname," he said.

"Maybe his mother remarried," she said, tutting and shaking her head.

Scotland Yard was called and they sent an officer who took down the names of J Ryan and Mrs Hanratty but as there was nothing to link this man to the murder it was not followed up.

CHAPTER FIVE

The police put out an appeal to boarding house keepers to report any strange or suspicious guests.

The manager of a hotel was suspicious of a man staying there so he phoned Scotland Yard.

"Hello," he said. "I saw your appeal on television regarding suspicious guests. Well I'm the manager of the Alexandra Court Hotel and I have a guest who's been locked in his room for five days."

"Is he still there?" the detective asked.

"Yes," he replied. "As I said, he's locked himself in his room."

"Someone will be with you right away," he said.

Within less than half an hour two detectives arrived at the hotel.

The manager took them to the man's room.

Thump, thump.

The vibrating sound of knuckles pounding against the wooden door of the hotel room penetrated through the walls.

Thump, thump.

Slowly the man inside turned off the radio and leaned closer to make sure he wasn't imagining the sound.

Thump, thump.

The door creaked open and the man stood facing the two detectives.

"We're looking for a Frederick Durrant," one of the detectives said. "He's listed as occupying this room."

"I'm Frederick Durrant," he replied.

"We'd like to have a word with you," the detective continued. "May we come in?"

"Certainly," he replied. "What is it you want?"

They went inside.

"Have you any ID?" the other detective asked.

"I have my driving license," he replied.

"Could I see it?" he asked.

"It's a bit difficult," he replied.

"Why is it difficult?" the detective asked.

"You see," the man replied. "My real name is Peter Alphon but I signed the register as Frederick Durrant."

"Why did you do that?" asked the detective, raising his eyebrows. "Are you hiding something?"

"No," replied the man.

"It sounds very suspicious to me," said the other detective. "You sign in using a false name then you lock yourself in your room for five days. What or who are you hiding from?"

"I'm not hiding from anybody," he replied.

Peter Alphon was a drifter surviving on an inheritance and the proceeds of gambling and his father was a senior figure at Scotland Yard.

"Can I ask you where you were on the evening of the 22nd of August?" the detective asked.

"I spent that evening with my mother," he replied. "And the next night I stayed in a scruffy doss house in Maida Vale."

"What's the name of the doss house?" the detective asked.

"The Vienna Hotel," he replied. "Why are you asking me all of these questions? I've done nothing wrong."

"We're investigating a murder," he replied. "We put out an appeal to hotels and guest houses asking the management to report any strange or suspicious guests and my lad you fall into that category. If you say what you are saying is correct then you have nothing to worry about."

The police checked this out and he was released.

Nearly three weeks after the shooting, hotel manager Robert Crocker was busy inspecting the rooms of the Vienna hotel.

He arrived at room 24, a large basement room with multiple beds. It was unoccupied at the time. On one of the armchairs which was in an alcove next to a single bed were two 38 calibre cartridge cases. Robert's first thought was to simply throw them away, but he decided to call his local police and report the finding. Scotland Yard confirmed that the cartridges matched those fired from the A6 murder weapon. Hotel records were checked to see who had stayed in room 24 when Michael Gregsten and Valerie story were abducted.

Being in the basement, room 24 was not often used. It was mainly given to travellers when the other rooms were booked out. As such only two people had stayed there recently. One was a man who had given his name as Frederick Durant. The other man, J. Ryan had stayed in room 24 on August 21st, the night before the shooting.

The police made a public appeal for Peter Alphon to contact them. As a result he voluntarily presented himself to them on 23rd September. He had already been interviewed on 27th August and 7th September. He was now the prime suspect for the murder.

He was put on two identity parades.

The first one was on 23rd September, held at Cannon Row Police Station, when Edward Blackall, James Trower, and Harold Hirons – the garage attendant who served the Morris Minor with two gallons of petrol about midnight on the night of the murder.

The second one was held at Guy's Hospital, London where the paralysed Valerie Storie failed to pick him out. In fact, she went straight past him and picked an innocent airman who was there just to make up the numbers.

He was released.

The police now focused on the occupant in the Vienna Hotel before Alphon.

Although his family's council flat in St. John's Wood, North London, was compact. Charles France always opened the door to his good friend Jim Ryan, whenever Jim needed a place to stay and Wednesday, August 30, 1961 was one such occasion. 24 year old Jim slept on the sofa in the sitting room, as he did every time he visited. Although the France family didn't know much about Jim's background, he was an exceptional house guest, tidy, polite and friendly.

Charles's wife, Charlotte, thought of Jim as a son, her three daughters called him uncle and loved it when he came to stay, as he spoiled them with chocolates, flowers, and pocket money. During his most recent stay, Jim Ryan joined Charles and Charlotte France in the sitting room where the couple were watching television, suddenly an alert flashed on the screen. Police were seeking an unidentified man for questioning in relation to the murder. The alert was accompanied by a sketch, known as an identikit, of the wanted man. The image showed a man with a pale face, slicked back, dark hair, deep set, brown eyes and bushy eyebrows. His right eyebrow was raised giving him a somewhat inquisitive expression. While studying the sketch, Charlotte France remarked that it looked like her house guest, Jim Ryan, the only exception being that Jim had blue eyes. Jim heard Charlotte, but said nothing keeping his eyes fixed to the television.

It had been a month since the A6 shooting and Charlotte had a growing suspicion towards someone she knew. She noted the likeness and suspected striking similarities.

She came forward to the police to formally implicate Jim in the crime. She also revealed his full name - James Hanratty.

Twenty five year old James Hanratty was a seasoned petty criminal. At the age of fifteen he began dabbling in minor crimes. By the age of eighteen he had been put on probation for a year after taking and driving a motor vehicle without consent. Two months later, he underwent a medical examination for national service but was denied entry on the grounds of being illiterate.

Following this he started breaking into houses and stealing property. He became adept at breaking into windows without being seen and wiping surfaces clean to remove his fingerprints. He was caught and served time in prison, where he tried to take his own life.

On October 5th, his luck changed. He was at one of his favourite local hangouts in Soho, The Rehearsal Club, when an acquaintance told him that officers were snooping around looking for him in relation to the A6 shooting.

Pale faced and panicky, he rang his good friend, Charles France. Charles tried to calm James telling him he had nothing to worry about and to go to Scotland Yard. Charles telephone line was being bugged by the police and he hadn't kept James on the line long enough that he could be traced. The following day, Hanratty phoned Scotland Yard from a public phone booth. He spoke to detective Acott explaining that he was innocent. However, he couldn't come forward as he was wanted for housebreaking after his fingerprints had been found at a crime scene a month earlier.

He told the detective he couldn't take another prison stint, but desperately wanted his alleged involvement in the A6 attack, cleared up.

He then called the newspaper officers of the Daily Mirror and spoke with an assistant editor. He explained his predicament and professed his innocence, telling the editor he had a watertight alibi for the night in question. Later that night, he made another call to Detective Acott telling the detective that he had spent the night of August 21st at the Vienna hotel under the alias, Jim Ryan, the next day, when the A6 attack took place; he had taken a train 200 miles north to Liverpool to stay with friends. He had been there for three nights before returning to London. He explained that the three men could testify for him, but they would not do so as they themselves were criminals.

Detectives drove to Liverpool and searched for anyone who might admit to being Hanratty's alibi. They had no luck.

The vehicles were crawling towards the promenade as Hanratty walked along Central Drive in Blackpool. His breath was leaving his mouth like the smoke was leaving the exhaust fumes of the cars as he pulled his collar up. Even the shimmering lights on the Blackpool Tower made it look as if it were shivering.

It was 11.15 pm on October 11th and walking towards the sea front was a thrill in itself – one that built with every step. There were lots of people about as the illuminations pulled in the tourists. He was confident he'd be safe here among them and away from the officers searching for him in London.

The Stevonia fish and chips cafe could have been any fish and chip establishment in Blackpool because they all looked the same. He decided to go into this particular one because just up the road he could see two police officers chatting to a group of ladies of the night.

The welcome scent of the fish and chips wafted through the air, calling to his frozen body to come and thaw out.

He entered the café and took a seat near the jukebox and looked for a waitress; the need for caffeine now consuming his mind.

She teetered over in a mini skirt and a top that left nothing to the imagination. Her heels were so impractical for someone who would have been on their feet all day, but she knew they made her legs look amazing.

Her face was fixed into a false smile. She had too much make up on and he doubted she could even remember the natural colour of her hair. She pulled a pencil from behind her ear and went through the routine questions she asks every customer that visits the café. She chewed her gum noisily between each word.

"I'll have fish and chips with mushy peas," he said. "And a coffee."

"Okay, sir," she replied, chewing on her gum like a cow chewing cud. "I'll bring it over to you."

As Detective Constables James Williams and Albert Stillings, the two police officers he'd seen outside, entered, he lowered his head.

"Two coffees love," Albert said to the waitress.

They stood at the counter drinking them.

When Hanratty had finished his meal he left. As he got outside, he felt a hand. It was Detective Constable Williams.

"I'm placing you under arrest," he said. "I have reason to believe you are James Hanratty and are wanted in connection with the A6 murder."

"Who?" he asked. "I don't know what you're talking about. My name is Bates. Peter Bates." "

"You'll have to accompany us to the police station," the detective replied. "Anything you say may be taken down and used in evidence."

On arriving at Blackpool Police Station he confessed to being James Hanratty.

CHAPTER SIX

Valerie had made a mistake at the identity parade but she realised what a shock the man who was guilty would get when he read that she was still alive. She, a woman he had raped and outraged, a woman he had left for dead, was living and she could send him to the death cell.

That morning, through the pain, she heard policemen's voices and saw the doctors leaning over her. She began to tell her fantastic story.

Miraculously, she could remember every detail. Because she was paralysed this took most of the shock and she was able to tell her story quite coherently. She knew that she was the one person in the world who could start the search for the man who murdered Mike and send him to the gallows for the terrible evil he had done.

He must have realised that too. Soon anonymous phone calls reached the hospital. They were calls that threatened her life. The curtains in her room were drawn. She was guarded day and night by police and dogs.

Every night her bed was moved to a different position in case somebody should try to shoot her through the window.

The policemen were wonderful. They were so patient, so understanding, so untiring and so human. She thought what a grand crowd they all were.

The days passed like dreams; muddled dreams of, "Oh no, no, don't shoot." Moments of waking up with fear gripping her; moments of an awful, inward anguish.

"Mike. Where is he now?" she thought. "What's happened to him?"

And then moments of memory, and the almost real feel of the coldness of his face, the blood and the sudden, dull explosion of a gun.

Two bullets had lodged in her body.

Before the police took them away, they let her see them.

She remembered vividly thinking, "How could those two tiny objects have caused so much pain and misery?" she thought. "Senseless, meaningless little lumps of lead. They've robbed me of Mike. Bullets. I never want to look at a bullet again."

Then came the letters; anonymous letters, vile, obscene letters. All that twisted world of rage and frustration which she never believed existed came flooding into her life.

She was a wicked woman. She had got what she deserved. She had wrecked a good man's life. They even wrote these things to her parents. Then, of course, there were letters of hope and encouragement and they came from all corners of the globe. The messages in them helped her a great deal. But the other letters just sickened her so she burned some and gave the police some.

She had thought of revenge and knew no pity for the murderer.

James Hanratty had been arrested and interviewed in Blackpool.

An identification parade was then arranged in Bedford.

At the identification parade held at Bedford Police Station on Friday 13th October, John Skillett, the driver of the car who had expressed concern about the way in which a Morris Minor had been driven in Gants Hill, identified James Hanratty as the driver. His passenger, Edward Blackhall, picked out a volunteer. James Trower, who had seen a Morris Minor turn into Avondale Crescent, also identified James Hanratty.

The next morning, there was another identification parade but this time at Stoke Mandeville Hospital where Valerie Storie remained confined to bed. She was wheeled in her bed into a room set aside for the identification.

This was the moment she had waited for.

Her lips bore the semblance of a smile; just enough to show that she was enjoying her thoughts, whatever they may be.

This was the moment she would avenge Mike and avenge the horror which had become her life.

One by one she asked the men in the line to say six words, "Be quiet will you. I'm thinking."

When she came to the man who was number six, her heart missed a beat. She knew this was the man. For he said in a voice she could never forget, "I'm finking."

That was the accent of the man with the gun.

She looked into his eyes. She was helpless and paralysed in her bed, but she felt no fear. This man had done his worst for her. She savoured this moment.

She was pushed up and down the line and again she asked the man to repeat those six damaging words.

He knew she recognised him and he felt a rising tide of fear from head to toe.

She made him wait as he had made them wait. He stood there; his cold blue eyes flickered.

He stood there with his arms folded and a strangely quiet smile – almost a smug smile – on his face.

She saw the flutter in those curious staring eyes.

"He thinks I'm not sure," she thought to herself. "Well, let him think. Let him hold on to hope."

Like a mesmerised rabbit she held him in the headlamps of her gaze and saw hope come and go and then there was nothing; just the cold bright eyes of the man who had killed Mike.

The twenty minutes allowed for the identification parade had come to an end.

"Do you recognise anybody?" Superintendent Acott asked.

Looking at the man again, her cold stare transforming into a powerful hatred, she quietly said, "Number six."

The sound of the door slamming shut behind her echoed around the corridor. Superintendent Acott gripped her arm and said, "Well done."

CHAPTER SEVEN

She had identified Hanratty, the man who murdered Mike and raped and shot her. She had seen fear and hope flicker in those cold, staring blue eyes. She had waited for twenty minutes knowing that this man who had trampled her life underfoot like a worm was suffering in that empty thing he no doubt called his soul.

Yet he still had to die. And she still had to get the threads of her life together again and become herself again.

She looked forward with no pity to the trial and wanted to settle her score with him. She wanted him to die because she knew he was guilty and this man must be punished for the evil things he had done. Why should mercy be shown to the man who had murdered Mike? The rape was almost unimportant and incidental in the rage she felt for the man who had taken the life of her lover.

Mike, the guy with the happy, boyish look whose gentle voice had wooed her and exchanged all sorts of confidence with her. Why should she pity that evil killer, mad though he may be, with his cold, blue, bulbous eyes?

In the hospital, at Stoke Mandeville, she struggled to get fit - or as fit as she could ever hope to be. She learned to swim in the hospital baths. She shot on the archery range from her wheelchair. She played table tennis. She spent her hours in the therapy department learning to balance and sit up just like a baby.

The difficulties arose when all she could feel were her head and shoulders floating in the air and having no idea where her feet were.

Then came the day when she stood up for the first time since the tragedy. She felt ten feet tall. Everyone was willing her on and she couldn't let them down. She was determined that nothing should stop her giving evidence against Mike's killer. She remembered reading somewhere that someone once said that pain was not cumulative - that if one man suffered pain he suffered as much pain as if a hundred thousand men suffered pain. There must be a limit.

She had passed over that limit and now horror and revulsion had turned into a cold realisation that this thing had happened. It was something she had to live with. Other people could have their love affairs and no one interfered. No one was ever any the wiser. But a man with a gun on Dead Man's Hill had changed all that. All the little intimacies of life which make up love and being for all of them had been blown to bits that night.

It seemed pretty silly to use the usual, conventional words to describe how she felt. She had long since passed the point of horror.

On 14th October, after the identification by Valerie Storie, James Hanratty was charged with murder but that was not the end of the evidence to become available for the prosecution. On 22nd November 1961, a prison officer overheard a prisoner Roy Langdale talking to another prisoner on the bus taking them to court. He reported the conversation to the Governor; this led to an approach by the police. Langdale's evidence was to the effect that he had exercised with James Hanratty and become friendly with him. During the course of their conversations, James Hanratty eventually talked about the murder, denying, but then admitting responsibility, going on to discuss the circumstances in terms only consistent with guilt. Needless to say, Roy Langdale was a man with a criminal record and there were some discrepancies between his statement and the evidence which he gave. The confession was challenged in its entirety.

Andy Williams was singing Moon River as she imagined the frosty spikes hanging from the window sill like a phantom's glassy fingers. She could smell the pine of the tree wafting through the room, mixing with the aroma of the turkey sizzling on tin foil. She could see the star flash of tinsel glittering brightly and orange ribbons of flame dancing in the hearth. But this was all in her imagination.

This was the time for spending with family and friends whether it's decorating the Christmas tree, wrapping the presents, cooking the dinner or watching TV – it's the time of year when people want to be at home surrounded by their loved ones.

The hospital staff had done their best to make the ward festive but it still wasn't the same and she felt a pang of homesickness. She missed the quiet homely celebrations she always had.

Four weeks later, towards the end of January, the trial started, and the trial that was to become the longest in British criminal history.

CHAPTER EIGHT

Four weeks later on January 22nd, at Bedford Assizes, the trial started; the trial that was to become the longest in British criminal history.

The judge was Sir William Gorman QC, the prosecution was Graham Swanwick QC, and the defence was a junior barrister Michael Sherrard.

Only one charge had been brought against Hanratty and that was the murder of Michael Gregsten.

This was the normal procedure at the time in cases involving capital murder but which allowed for the evidence relating to Valerie's attack to be placed before the jury. The case centred on the evidence of identification of Hanratty not only by Valerie Storie but also by the witnesses who saw the Morris Minor being driven recklessly.

The outcome of the A6 murder trial would be decided by a jury of eleven, not twelve people, because one of the jury members became sick every time he heard the word blood mentioned.

Valerie was called to give evidence on January 23rd, the second day of the trial. She dressed carefully in her best tartan slacks and a yellow sweater ready for her ride in the ambulance. She wanted Hanratty to see that she had won through. Somehow it seemed important for Mike's sake that she should seem proud and confident in their victory – that's how she regarded this trial.

She was pushed into court in a wheelchair accompanied by a nurse, a therapist and a woman police officer.

In the impressive court room she knew she made a bright splash of colour among the black gowns and grey wigs and the blue police uniforms. Valerie Storie, the woman, was coming to life again.

A murmuring buzz passed through the public gallery as she told the court her name and address.

With the formalities over, she started answering questions about the events of that horrible night.

Graham Swanwick asked her to tell the court everything in detail about that night.

"That evening, Michael had come for tea and we left to go to the pub in Taplow to have a drink and make plans for a motor rally," she said. "The pub started to get busy so we decided to drive to a place not far away which we knew well. We had been chatting in the car for about half an hour when someone tapped on the car window."

She then went into detail of the hours of terror they had endured as they were held up at gunpoint and robbed. She explained how the gunman had wanted to put Michael in the boot but had been persuaded otherwise. She spoke about the journey through Slough, Middlesex and on to the A6 in great detail, the stopping for cigarettes and petrol and how on numerous occasions she had tried to frustrate the gunman. She explained how they had tried to attract attention by switching the car's reversing light on and off.

"It seemed that he didn't have any particular plan," she continued. "And he repeatedly warned us not to turn around and look at him." In graphic detail she spoke of the moment Michael was shot twice in the head at point-blank range and with tears streaming down her face, she told the part of the story where all she could hear was the sound of blood pouring from his head. She said that this was the first time she screamed out.

She turned and looked directly at Hanratty in the dock and with nostrils flaring she said, 'You shot him, you bastard.'

She saw his expression change and her heart gave a little flutter. So he was human after all and now he was cracking. Now he wasn't so cocky. Now there was a look of fear.

Yes it was happening to him. The certainty that horror was about to envelop him as he had made it envelop them on Dead Man's Hill was sweeping over James Hanratty.

When he looked back at her she felt no emotion.

She then told the court of how she was forced into the back of the car and raped. She described how she was made to drag Michael's bloodstained body from the car and how she begged the gunman to let her go before he shot her.

"Could you explain to the court how you came to pick out an innocent man on the first identification parade?" Mr. Swanwick asked. "Yet on the second, when the accused was present, you were absolutely sure it was him. Had you any doubt at the time?"

"I had no doubt at all that this was the man who shot Mike and me," she replied.

"Have you any doubt now?" he asked.

"I have no doubt whatsoever," she replied.

It was now the turn of Michael Sherrard to question what Valerie had just told the court.

His client's defence was that he was not the man in the back of the car that night, and therefore, Valerie Storie was wrong in her identification.

"Miss Storie, I want you to understand quite clearly that I am in no way attempting to belittle the horrifying experience you underwent or the magnitude of the tragedy which overtook you," he said. "I am sure your courage must be admired by everyone, but you will appreciate, on the other hand, my plain duty to my client is to attempt to save his life and indeed to see that he is not imperilled on anything other than the basis of objective evidence and objective evidence alone."

"Yes," she replied.

"The Morris Minor you had been in that night had somehow been hotted up because of its use in rallying and that, coupled with the fact that it had a leaky exhaust, made it much noisier than otherwise would have been the case. If the noise in the car was so loud, wasn't it just likely that much of what was said between the three of you was only part heard or perhaps misunderstood?"

"The car had not been adapted in any way," she replied. "And the leaking exhaust made no difference to the sound of the engine at all."

"Where did you purchase the cigarettes that night?" he asked.

"Stanmore," she replied.

"When I questioned you before," he said. "You said you had purchased them at Harrow, now you're saying it was Stanmore."

"To me they are the same place," she said. "They are simply urbanised areas that border each other."

"You said that my client warned you about some roadworks in the area inferring that he knew the area well," he said. "I suggest that there had been an advanced warning sign of the roadworks and that was how he knew there would be some just around the corner."

"I'm afraid your suggestion is wrong," she said. "There were no advanced warnings of the roadworks."

He continued to probe her ability to accurately recall conversations on the night. He was particularly interested in her use of the word 'institutions' when she described what the gunman had said about his criminal history. At one stage she used the word and then she referred to it directly as 'borstal training'. Which had been correct? Once more, she said she had used both terms to describe what she had been told; they were interchangeable as far as she was concerned.

"Let's turn our attention to the young man who found you at the roadside," he said. "You told him that you had given your attacker a lift and that his hair was light in colour."

"Hardly that," she said. "And I told him that the attacker had dark brown hair."

"Can you acknowledge that you only had a momentary glimpse of your attacker's face when the passing car's headlights had lit it up?" he asked.

"Yes," she replied. "This was the only real proper glimpse of him that I had."

"All I can say," he said. "That if a witness only has a fleeting look, a second or two in

a dark environment under such stressful conditions, their evidence must be viewed with caution."

Sherrard told the court that his client was five feet eight inches tall and that Miss Storie had described her attacker as slightly taller than herself. She was five feet three and a half inches tall in flat shoes. For almost all of the five hours that she had been held captive, the hijacker had been sitting in the back of the car. The only time when she saw him standing up was when he got out of the car to force her into the back seat before he raped her and the other was when she was pulling her boyfriend's dead body from the car with the gunman standing over her. Sherrard was also very interested in the identity parades. The first one in which Peter Alphon had taken part in was dealt with directly. She had made a mistake, although she added that she did not realise that the men were allowed to speak, something that had been made available to her at the second in which Hanratty had been present. The point had been made, though, that Valerie was human and fallible. Matters for the defence were helped by the fact that after the Alphon parade, she had seen a photograph of him in the national newspapers and had commented to a doctor that he did resemble her attacker. Sherrard's questioning now came to an end.

"Miss Storie," he said. "One appreciates your position of course, but it is my plain duty to suggest to you, that although you may be convinced in your own mind, you are nevertheless absolutely honest, but absolutely wrong. I must make that quite plain to you."

"I do not agree with that suggestion," she replied.

Graham Swanwick had a few further questions for her but finished his re-examination by asking, "Have you any doubt whatever about your identification?"

"I have no doubt at all," she replied.

Examination and cross-examination complete, Valerie had been in the witness box for almost three hours spread over two days.

CHAPTER NINE

The trial continued and John Kerr, the young man who found Valerie Storie and Michael Gregsten, took the stand.

"Could you tell the court in your own words what you witnessed on the morning of August 23rd?" Mr Swanwick asked.

"I saw that Miss Storie was alive and badly injured," he replied. "I asked her if she was all right and what had happened. She said that they had been held up by a gunman around nine thirty the previous evening. I wrote down everything she told me because I didn't think she was going to live."

"Is this the document that you wrote this information on?" Mr Swanwick asked, handing him a piece of paper.

"Yes sir," he replied.

Three more important witnesses followed.

John Skillett, Edward Blackhall and James Trower, the three men who had witnessed the irregular driving of the Morris Minor in Ilford just a few hours after the murder.

John Skillett said that he had seen the car being driven badly and had positively identified Hanratty as the driver and James Trower said that he had also seen the car being driven badly and had afterwards picked out Hanratty on an identification parade.

"Did my client's ginger-coloured hair distract you when you identified him?" Mr Sherrard asked John Skillett.

"It wasn't an issue," he replied. "I was looking at the faces of the men. The police told me that one of the men may be responsible for the A6 murder. I was worried about it and the face of the man I saw driving the car was a face I would never forget."

"It seems strange that you can remember the face of the man driving the car," Mr Sherrard continued. "But you never noticed the red strips on the rear bumper of the car in the same way as your passenger did. It is my duty to put it to you that in fact you made a most serious mistake in your identification."

"No sir," Mr Skillett said.

James Trower was also asked about the distinctive coloured of Hanratty's hair at the parade, but he dismissed it out of hand. He said he hadn't even thought about the hair colour and it was the man's face he was interested in. He said that he knew a man's life was at stake but he had no doubt that Hanratty was the man who was driving the car.

His position was supported by the fact that he had attended the earlier identification parade when Alphon was taking part and he had not selected anyone. He had only picked out one man and that was Hanratty.

The last of the three witnesses was Edward Blackhall. He had seen the red strips and the green sticker on the back of the car as it sped along Eastern Avenue that morning but on each of the identification parades, he had picked out someone not involved in the investigation. In fact, Mr Sherrard accused him of casually walking into two identification parades and regarding them as a children's party game.

The trial the continued with the jury hearing about the finding of the gun on the bus and the empty cartridges found at the Vienna Hotel and statements from witnesses including the manager of the guest house where the cartridges were found, and Mr and Mrs France, James Hanratty's close friends.

CHAPTER TEN

The time had at last come for the accused man, James Hanratty, to take his place in the witness box. So far, the jury had heard only from the prosecution that he was the killer.

"I am a convicted thief and lived with my parents until July last year," he told the jury. "I have been committing break-ins all last summer and called myself Jimmy Ryan. I dyed my natural auburn hair to make me look less obvious. I made friends with Louise Anderson, who owns an antique shop and did sell stolen jewellery to her. I also looked on the France family as my own family."

He admitted that he had told Charles France that he hid his unwanted jewellery under the seats of buses, and since coming out of prison in March he had stayed with both of them on a number of occasions.

He went into detail about his movements on the days leading up to the killing, saying that on Sunday, 20th August he had told the France family that he intended to go to Liverpool to sell the property he had stolen in a break-in.

On the Monday night he had stayed in the basement room of the Vienna hotel, had occupied the single bed in the alcove of the room and left the hotel the following morning after breakfast. He then walked to Paddington railway station to catch the train to Liverpool before realising his error and so took a taxi to Euston when he eventually boarded the train around midday; he shared a compartment with a man who he was able to describe in some detail.

He arrived at Liverpool around 4.30 p.m. He had a wash and brush-up at the station and a cup of tea in the station buffet before dropping his case off in the left luggage office with a man whose hand was deformed in some way.

"Why did you go to Liverpool?" Mr Sherrard asked.

"I stole a gold watch from a house in Harrow," he replied. "And I went to Liverpool to see if I could sell it."

"Liverpool seems a long way to go to sell a stolen watch," said Mr Sherrard.

"I have friends there," he said. "I was going to visit them and thought that whilst I was there I could sell the watch. I walked into town and had a cup of tea in Lyon's café in Lime Street. I tried to sell the watch to a bloke standing at the bottom of some stairs leading up to a billiard hall. He refused to buy it so I was making grounds to go upstairs, when the man called me back and told me not to go in as he didn't want stolen property being sold inside the premises."

"What do you mean when you say making grounds to go upstairs?" the Judge asked.

"I meant I started to make my way up the stairs," he replied.

His story so far was more or less the same of what he had told Detective Acott during his interviews.

He then went into detail about his trip to Rhyl and Mr Sherrard directed him to tell the jury in detail all he could remember, no matter how unimportant it may seem.

For the first time, the prosecution heard his new alibi.

He said he went to Rhyl to interview a man called Terry Evans.'

"It was dark when I got there," he said. "I asked five or six people for directions to a bed and breakfast. After some time, I found one. The house had a B&B sign in the window and the woman who answered the door was about fifty years old and of average build. She wore glasses and had grey hair. I went up a flight of stairs and stayed in a room on the second floor at the back of the house. Once I was in the room I didn't draw the curtains because it was at the back and I could hear trains shunting. I saw a green bath in the top part of the property, which I guess was the attic. I didn't have to check in. I paid one pound five shillings to stay two nights." Hanratty said that having stayed the night in the bed and breakfast on the night of 22nd and 23rd August, he spent the next day trying to find Evans. He had no luck, stayed another night in the boarding house and returned the following day to Liverpool. He still hadn't sold his stolen jewellery. He left his case in the left luggage office again, had a meal and then went to see the film *The Guns of Navarone*.

Mr Sherrard asked him to tell the jury of anything else he could remember about his activities in Liverpool.

"Well, I have studied this very carefully and the most important factors of what I can remember was a boxing match," he said. "I'm very interested in boxing but I couldn't get any tickets because they had sold out. I went to the Exchange hotel near Lime Street Station and sent a telegram to Dixie France. I then went to New Brighton for the evening. Later that night I got a train back to London and arrived about five or six in the morning."

Mr Sherrard emphasised how being in Rhyl made it impossible for Hanratty to have committed the murder. Mr Swanwick began his cross-examination.

"Why didn't you tell the police the truth about your trip to Rhyl?" he asked.

"I didn't tell Superintendent Acott," Hanratty replied. "Because at that point I didn't know the name of the street, the number of the house or even the name of the people living in the house. At that stage I knew that I was only wanted for interviewing, not for the actual A6 murder, which I eventually found out later, or the truth would have been told straight away. I know I made a terrible mistake by telling

Superintendent Acott about these three men but I have been advised that the truth only counts in this matter and what I have said here, every word of it, is the truth. I am a man with a prison record and I know in such a trial of this degree that it is very vital for a man once to change his evidence in such a serious trial, but I know inside of me somewhere, in Rhyl this house does exist, and by telling the truth these people will come to my assistance."

"If what you are saying about Rhyl is true," Mr Swanwick asked. "Then why didn't you go back to Rhyl and find the people who could support your story instead of staying in Liverpool?"

"Because when I went to Liverpool I didn't have the right bearings of Rhyl as I had only been there on two occasions," he replied. "Though I did stay there two nights, I have some idea of the house I stayed in and some description."

Once he had learned that he was wanted by the police and had spoken to Superintendent Acott on the telephone, he stole a Mk VII Jaguar from Portland Place in London and drove it to Oldham, where he abandoned it and caught the train to Liverpool.

Hanratty had been in the witness box for most of the day.

CHAPTER ELEVEN

With all the evidence concluded, both sides summed up their cases to the jury. Mr Sherrard stood up and walked to the jury box.

Pausing and looking at his client in the dock, "This crime was committed by a local maniac probably sleeping rough in a field," he said. "The description of the gunman could fit any one of a number of people and the killer's supposed profile doesn't match my client. Identification is the major fact and this is something so weak, so precarious that you should ignore," he continued. "Given Miss Storie's dreadful circumstances and her fleeting glimpse of the attacker, as well as her identifying an innocent person at the first identification parade, this makes her evidence wholly unreliable. You should dismiss the witnesses who saw the Morris Minor being driven that morning. They are simply wrong."

Now it was Mr Swanwick for the prosecution's turn.

"I want to deal with the red herrings that have appeared in these proceedings," he said. "Firstly, this crime was not committed by a local maniac sleeping rough in a field somewhere; the gunman had no local knowledge but it is clear that he knows the London area well. Secondly, there is absolutely no evidence that Mr Peter Alphon is involved and was eliminated from the investigation almost as soon as his name first appeared. Three people from three different locations identified the defendant. Miss Storie may have only had a fleeting glimpse of her attacker but she heard his voice for over five hours."

He made his way to the front of the court.

"She picked out the wrong man on the first identification parade but only took eleven minutes to pick out the prisoner and not twenty minutes as claimed by the defence counsel. Once the defendant realised that Miss Storie was still alive he knew he needed a false alibi to save him from the hangman's noose." Walking towards the defendant's counsel and with one finger high in the air he continued even louder, "Where does all this lead? In which direction does the evidence point? In my submission, it leads and points inevitably to one conclusion and one conclusion only; the guilt of the accused," he said, and with full force slammed his hand down on the defendant counsel's desk.

The crowd in the public gallery gasped.

The Judge, Mr Justice Gorman's summing up lasted for ten hours spread over three days. Before the jury retired he made his final comments.

"You, the jury, need to look at this case coolly, objectively and with no hint of emotion," he said. "It must have been agonising for Miss Storie to give evidence but let us forget this sorry picture. The tragic picture of a woman whose life has been blasted."

Before retiring the jury members asked if they could have a copy of the court transcript, which would have amounted to nearly one thousand three hundred pages of evidence.

"There are certain passages in the transcript which took place the absence of the jury and these matters clearly would have to be removed from the transcript if the application is acceded to," said Mr Swanwick QC.

"I will therefore have to refuse this request," said the Judge. "But you can have a copy of the list of witnesses."

Looking across at counsel for defence and prosecuting counsel, "I want the jury to have every exhibit in the case in their room while they deliberate," he said. The one hundred and thirty six items, including the revolver which Crown said was the murder weapon, were carried to the jury's room from the Court.

Slowly, almost hesitantly, the jury began to rise. Awkwardly, they filed out of the jury box and left the Court.

The police officer opened the door to a large unpleasant looking room furnished with a long conference table and a dozen chairs. It smelled damp and the walls needed a fresh covering of paint. The one window looked out across the staff car park; above it was an old clock. On the right hand side was a toilet. Bottles of water, notepads, pencils, and ashtrays lay on the table. As the police officer held the door open, slowly, almost self-consciously, the eleven members of the jury filed in. He counted them as they entered the room.

"Okay gentlemen," he said. "If there's anything you want just knock on the door. I'll be right outside."

He closed the door and they heard the sound of it being locked.

"I didn't know that we were being locked in," said juror number two.

"Yes, they lock the door," said number three. "What did you think?"

"Well, let's get started," he said, "The sooner this is over the better."

"What did you think of the case?" juror four asked.

"I found it very interesting," replied number seven. "I thought the prosecuting counsel was very sharp, the way he attacked the defendant."

"I think he knew what he was on about," said number eleven.

"Now you can handle this any way you want," said the foreman. "I'm not going to make any rules. If we want to talk about it first and then vote, that's one way. Or we can vote right now to see how we stand. That's all I have to say."

"Let's just vote," said number seven. "Then we can all go home."

"That's your choice," said the foreman. "But remember we've got a murder charge here. If we all vote guilty we're sending a man to the gallows. That's the law."

"I think we all know that," said number six.

"Come on, let's vote," said number three.

"Is there anybody who doesn't want to vote?" the foreman asked, as he looked at them.

The others remained silent.

"Okay. There are only eleven of us so it has to be an eleven to nothing vote either way," the foreman said. "That's the law. Are we ready? Those voting guilty raise your hands."

Six hands went up immediately. Then slowly, the others raised their hands.

Everybody looked around the table as the foreman got up and began to count the hands. All hands were raised except for juror number ten.

"Eight....nine...ten. That's ten for guilty," the foreman said. "Okay. Not guilty."

The tenth juror raised his hand.

"One," said the foreman. Okay ten to one guilty. Now we know where we are."

He sat back down.

"So what do we do now?" asked juror number seven.

"I suppose we have to talk about it," replied juror number eight.

Number four looked at number ten and asked, "Do you really think he's innocent?"

"I don't know," he replied.

"Let's be reasonable," said number four. "You heard the same things as we did in the Court. The man's a dangerous killer. You can see it."

"It's obvious he's guilty," said number seven. "I was convinced from day one."

"Well, who wasn't?" asked number four. "I think this is an open and shut case. The prosecution proved it in a dozen different ways. Do you want me to jog your memory?"

"No," replied number ten.

"Then what do you want?" asked number three.

"Nothing," he replied. "I just want us to talk about it."

"What's there to talk about?" asked number seven. "Ten men here agree. Nobody had to think twice about it except you."

"Let me ask you something," said number three. "Do you believe his story?"

"I don't know whether or not I believe him," he replied. "Perhaps I don't."

"So why did you vote not guilty?" asked number seven.

"There are ten votes for guilty," he replied. "It isn't easy for me to raise my hand and send a man off to die without talking about it first."

"You couldn't change my mind if you talked all day long," said number four.

"I'm not trying to change your mind," he said. "We're talking about somebody's life here. We can't decide in five minutes. What if we're wrong?"

"Wrong?" number four asked. "He didn't think about the life of his victim when he shot him in cold blood."

There was a quiet that was deafening.

"Has anybody got anything else to say?" asked the foreman.

"I think we should ask the Judge for a clarification about reasonable doubt," replied number ten.

"I think that's a good point," the foreman said. "We have a job to do. Maybe the gentleman who's disagreeing might have a change of mind with the Judge's guidance."

The policeman heard the knock on the door. The jurors heard the key turn in the lock and the door opened.

"Are you ready?" the policeman asked.

"Not yet," replied the foreman. "Can you give the Judge this note?"

It had been six hours and twenty minutes since the jury had left and now the Court reassembled again.

The atmosphere was tense with more than eighty police officers, counsel and newspaper reporters who had been pacing the entrance hall, which had now become a carpet of cigarette ends under their feet.

The Hanratty family were gathered together awaiting the outcome of their son's fate while outside hundreds of people were hanging around like a bad smell and would still be there until they heard the verdict.

"I have received a note from the jury," said the Judge. "I will read out what it says: May we have a further statement from you regarding the definition of reasonable doubt?" he continued. "I have never used the phrase reasonable doubt as it often leads to confusion but my answer is this. If you have a reasonable doubt you cannot be sure and therefore you may think the best way of looking at it is this: you have to be sure of the guilt of the accused before you find him guilty."

The Court broke up again.

The police officer returned to the jury with the Judge's answer.

"Here's what I think and I'm talking facts," said juror number four. "Let's look at the survivor who was also a victim in this case. She didn't get a good look at her attacker but she'd been in his company for over five hours and recognised his voice when he spoke at the ID parade."

"And the guy first said he was in Liverpool at the time of the murder," said number five. "He then changed his alibi and said he was in Rhyl. Those are the facts. You can't refute facts."

"It's obvious to me anyway that the man's entire story is flimsy," said number three.

"He claimed he was in Liverpool and now claims he was in Rhyl."

"We can talk about this forever," said number seven. "I mean, look at the guy's record. He's been in and out of the nick since he was a teenager. He bragged about hiding stolen property under the back seat of a bus. That's where they found the gun and ammunition. He told the victims his name was Jim. He said he felt like a cowboy having a gun. The man's a psychopath."

"We're her to decide whether he's guilty or innocent of murder," said number five.

"Not to go into reasons about his background."

"Okay, okay, let's stop all this arguing," said the foreman. "We're wasting time." He pointed to juror number ten and said, "It's your turn." "I wasn't expecting a turn," he said, raising his eyebrows. "I thought you were all supposed to be convincing me to change my mind."

"Look," said the foreman. "I'm sure we're all hungry. I know I am. Maybe we can sort this out over a meal. Let's ask the Judge if we can eat."

He knocked on the door again and gave another note to the police officer.

The Court reassembled again at about 7.30 pm.

The Judge sat waiting while Hanratty was told it was necessary for him to return to the dock.

"Could I be excused to go below to the cell and explain the situation to my client?"

Mr Sherrard asked the Judge. "I think it is causing him some distress, this constant...."

The Judge interrupting, said, "Yes, I must have him here."

After Hanratty had stepped into the dock the Judge said," I have received another note from the jury. This time it says is it possible for us to have some tea, please?"

He looked at both counsel and asked, "Do either of you have any objection to this?"

They both said they had none.

"That being so," the Judge observed. "Arrangements have already been made but I wasn't going to allow it to be carried out until I had the consent of both of you." Hanratty was taken back to his cell.

The jury had a meal of cold meat, salad, peaches and cream while they continued discussing whether Hanratty should live or die.

"If you want me to tell you how I feel about it right now," said number ten. "It's okay with me."

"Do what you think fit," said the foreman.

"I only know as much as you do," number ten continued. "According to the prosecution the man is guilty. Maybe he is. I sat there in court for twenty one days listening while the evidence built up. Everybody sounded so positive but I got a gut feeling that the defence counsel wasn't doing his job. There was one eye witness to the killing. Suppose she was wrong."

"What do you mean, suppose she was wrong?" asked number six.

"Could she be wrong?" number ten asked.

"She took the stand on oath," replied number six. "What are you trying to say?"

"She's only human," he replied. "People make mistakes. Could she be wrong?"

"I don't think so," replied number six.

"Do you know so?" he asked.

"Nobody can know a thing like that," he replied.

"Look," said number seven. "The woman saw him shoot the victim in cold blood.

What more do you want?"

"Okay, let's have a secret vote," said number four.

"Right," said the foreman. "There's another vote called for. Are there any objections?"

"It's okay," said number ten. "There's no need for a secret vote I have no doubt now so I'll go along with the rest of you and vote guilty."

"Let's have a show of hands then," said the foreman. "Those voting guilty raise your hands."

All hands went up.

The foreman knocked on the door for the last time.

"Are you ready?" the police officer asked.

"We're ready," he replied.

"All right gentlemen, come along."

By 9.10 pm the jury had reached a decision and the Court reassembled for the last

time.

The loudest sound in the Court at this moment was the sound of silence.

"Members of the jury have you reached your verdict?" the Judge asked.

"Yes, your honour we have," replied the foreman.

"Members of the jury, on the case of the Crown versus James Hanratty, what do you say?" the Judge asked. "Your honour, the members of this jury find the defendant guilty," he replied.

Loud conversation burst out within the Court.

The sound of the gavel hammering on the bench several times reverberated through the Court.

"Order, order in my court," said the Judge.

There was peace and calm once more.

He looked at James Hanratty and asked, "Is there anything you would like to say regarding why sentence of death should not be passed?"

The colour left his face and he found it difficult to talk. He snapped his fingers, and after a long pause he replied, "I am not innocent. I mean I am innocent, my Lord and I will appeal. That is all I have to say at this stage."

The Judge draped his black cloth over his wig and said, "James Hanratty, the sentence of this Court is that you suffer death in the manner authorised by law, and may God have mercy on your soul."

CHAPTER TWELVE

It was Michael Sherrard's duty to go down to the cells to see James Hanratty within minutes of the Judge having passed sentence.

Hanratty was handcuffed between two wardens.

Mr Sherrard approached him and before he could say anything Hanratty pulled his manacled hand forward and took his hand.

"You're not to upset yourself, sir, "he said. "We'll appeal."

"Yes we'll appeal," Mr Sherrard said.

The appeal failed.

He had spent six weeks in the condemned cell and it was the night before the execution.

He wrote a letter to his brother Michael.

"Well, Mick I am going to do my best to face the morning with courage and strength and I am sure God will give me the courage to do so," he wrote. "Mick now you are the eldest in the family and I know that I could not count on anybody better than yourself. Mick we always got on well together and we had many good times together over the years. But I am going to ask you to do me a small favour, that is I would like you to try and clear my name of this crime and one day they will venture again and then the truth will come out. Time is drawing near; it is almost daylight, so please look after Mum and Dad for me, Jimmy."

As he was writing the letter he felt a violent pain in his head, his body chilled and his forehead burning. He had convulsive trembling and from time to time the pen fell from his hand as if by galvanic shock.

Every time he got up, or bent forward, it felt as if there was a fluid floating in his head, which made his brain beat violently against his skull. HIs eyes stung as though full of smoke and his limbs ached.

"Only a few more hours," he thought. "And all this will be over. They say that it is nothing, that one does not suffer, and that it is an easy end; that death in this way is very much simplified.

Then, what do they call they call this agony of six weeks, this summing up in one day? What then is the anguish of this irreparable day, which is passing so slowly and yet so fast? What is this ladder of tortures which terminates on the scaffold? Are there any who have been killed in this way who have come back to give thanks and say: "It is a great invention. You can depend on it. The mechanism is perfect." No. Less than a minute, less than a second, and the thing is done. None have ever, except in mind, been in place of the one who is there, at the moment when the trapdoor falls, and the rope burns the flesh and breaks the neck."

Half an hour before his execution, a white haired man with a very gentle look entered. James was bewildered and scarcely heard what Father Hulme, the priest, was saying. His words seemed useless and Hanratty remained indifferent. The words glided away like the drops of rain on the window panes of his cell.

Nevertheless, the priest's appearance made him feel good and he felt an ardent thirst for the good and consoling words.

When they were sitting down, the priest on a chair, and Hanratty on the bed, the priest said, "My son ...."

This word opened Hanratty's heart.

"My son, do you believe in God?" he asked.

"Yes, father," he replied.

"Do you believe in the Holy Catholic, Apostolic and Roman Church?" he asked.

"Willingly," he replied.

"My son," he said, "you have an air of doubt."

Then he began to speak; he spoke a, long time; he uttered a quantity of words; then when he had finished, he got up, looked at Hanratty and said, "Well, are you guilty of the crime you have been sentenced to die for?"

Hanratty had listened to him with avidity at first, then with attention, then with devotion.

He got up, and said, "Sir, I am innocent, please leave me alone, I beg of you."

The priest withdrew in silence shaking his head.

James Hanratty was a Catholic and believed he would suffer eternal damnation if he died without confessing sins which he had not confessed at previous confessions. He sincerely accepted in his last hours the ministration of a Catholic priest to whom he could have confessed in the presence of God.

The hangman, Harry Allen, had been preparing for this controversial execution. He had taken a sneak look at the condemned man in the exercise yard. It was crucial for him to know the height and weight for a quick and painless death. Then he did a test using a sandbag, to see how much rope to use. If the drop was too long for the weight, it would pull the head off. The gallows stood in a small room next to the condemned cell. In the room were two beams and a crossbar with the rope dangling.

The time had come.

The hangman went to the cell.

"Good morning," he said, greeting the condemned man.

Hanratty was silent.

The hangman tied Hanratty's hands behind his back. The door to the execution chamber opened and Hanratty strutted onto the scaffold.

Royston Rickard, the hangman's assistant tied Hanratty's legs while the hangman placed the hood on his head and the rope around his neck.

In seconds the lever was pulled. The trap door fell open and Hanratty was gone.

The rope twisted on itself.

It was eight o' clock on the morning of April 4th 1962.

From walking from the condemned cell to Hanratty being confirmed dead took less than a minute.

He died instantly and painlessly.

The warder went back to the cell, looked at Hanratty's pyjamas lying folded on the bed and an empty cup of tea on the table and said, "We just killed a man."

That morning as Valerie Storie lay in her bed at Stoke Mandeville Hospital she wondered if Hanratty had experienced the terror that she and Michael had known that night in August. She prayed that God would have mercy on the soul of James

Hanratty. She felt great sympathy towards his parents.

"When a woman gives birth to a child does she know how life will shape that child?" she thought. "Once Hanratty had been a baby. In a queer way we were all part of the life cycle, the huge drama of living. Mike, me, James Hanratty, my parents, Hanratty's parents, Mike's wife, Mike's children thrown together. All of us loved and being loved. Yet one mad gene run amok in the shape of James Hanratty seemed like an ugly wave suddenly lurching up out of nothingness rejecting everything gentle and kind and pitying and making chaos and nonsense of the carefully woven loves of the other characters in our collective drama."

That was that. She lay back on her bed and knew that now life had to begin again for her. She knew that she may never walk again.

A bullet had passed through her spine. The doctors could not be sure whether the nerves were severed or just frayed. They told her it would take three years before they could discover the full extent of her injuries.

"Well, at least I am alive," she thought. "And I know now that nothing else I might be called upon to face could equal the thing that I have survived."

That thought alone gave her strength.

CHAPTER THIRTEEN

It began with a prayer then the grave-diggers got to work in a final gruesome attempt to end four decades of doubt.

As dawn broke, with the mist still swirling around the suburban cemetery in Hertfordshire, they exhumed the body of James Hanratty, the man hanged for the notorious A6 murder – thirty five years after it had been buried there.

One way or another, experts hoped to draw a line under the constant speculation over whether he carried out the 1961 murder. If he didn't, legal history would have to be rewritten and his conviction put down as one of the country's most disastrous miscarriages of justice.

Inside a large marquee at Carpender's Park Cemetery, near Watford, detectives stood side by side with grave-diggers, a pathologist, a fully-robed priest and some of Hanratty's relatives.

They said prayers in the cause of truth, justice and peace and sang hymns from a specially prepared order of service.

Cemetery staff removed the inscribed stone from his grave. 'Rest in Peace' were among the words on it - and no one there would have missed the irony.

Hanratty's last words to his family had made it clear he could have no peace without pardon.

So the digging began at 4 am. Just under four hours later, the coffin containing Hanratty's aunt was lifted. Annie Cunningham, who died in 1977, was buried on top of Hanratty and had to be exhumed with him.

It took a further ninety minutes or so before Hanratty could be lifted. This was the second time his resting place has been disturbed - his family moved him from an unconsecrated pit at Bedford Prison in 1966.

Since then he has lain not with killers, but among unfamiliar names on scores of gravestones beside oak and silver birch trees.

When the sound of the digging stopped emerging from the arc light-lit marquee, they had uncovered the coffin still intact. But now it was submerged in water.

Generator-driven pumps drowned out the dawn chorus. Shadows silhouetted against the white wall of the marquee danced around for a little longer.

The last time James Hanratty rode in a plain van with darkened windows, he had just been sentenced to death by a judge.

Now, in a private ambulance painted black, they took his remains to a mortuary. There, they removed small samples of bone for examination by the Forensic Science Service. DNA would be compared with that taken from Miss Storie's underwear.

The Crown argued that exhuming the body to get DNA samples directly was the only way to establish guilt or innocence without doubt. The Court of Appeal accepted it was 'in the interests of justice' to do so.

At first the Hanratty family objected to the exhumation on the grounds that his aunt's body would be disturbed.

Was this an excuse that after all these years the DNA results might prove that he was guilty after all?

Meanwhile the delicate balance of dignity versus necessity continued to border on the macabre at Carpender's Park.

Within a few hours, the main players in this event, now including Hanratty's brother Michael, returned with two new coffins containing the carefully-placed remains.

HANRATTY - THE FINAL CURTAIN

The sound of prayer and song filtered out once again from the marquee as Hanratty and his aunt were reburied.

A few months later, the DNA results pointed to Hanratty being the killer beyond any reasonable doubt but his family still argue that his DNA was found on Valerie Storie's underwear through cross contamination because his clothes and hers were carried to and from the Court in the same box.

CHAPTER FOURTEEN

The A6 murder shook Britain. It was an August evening in 1961 when Valerie Storie and Michael Gregsten sat in their Morris Minor car. The car was parked in a field. They were kidnapped at gun point, told to drive around for hours before their kidnapper shot Gregsten dead and then raped Valerie Storie before shooting her too.

It was a time of low crime and gun crime was all but unheard of. Eight months later an illiterate twenty five year old petty thief with psychiatric problems was sent hurtling through the trap door of the gallows. His name was James Hanratty. He had paid for the A6 murder. But was he guilty?

Michael Gregsten was married with two children. His marriage broke down. He and his wife lived separately. Thirty six year old Gregsten was a scientist and began an affair with a twenty two year old year old colleague named Valerie Storie.

On 22nd August 1961 the two went to a pub. Another person present in the pub was Peter Louis Alphon. He was a thirty one year old career criminal. Gregsten and Storie later got into a Morris Minor he had borrowed. They drove to an isolated field. There was no lighting around the area. There were no houses for a few hundred metres. There was a reason why this courting couple wanted privacy.

A knock on the window alerted them to the presence of a man. He wore a handkerchief over the lower part of his face and brandished a revolver. He told them he was a desperate man and demanded that he let them into the car.

Valerie told her lover to drive off. He decided not to. It was to cost him his life. The man got into the rear seat. He was dressed in a smart suit. He told them to drive off. They went on a wild goose chase around London and the Home Counties. The kidnapper seemed to have no idea where he wanted to go. He often changed his mind. He spoke almost incessantly. The gunman had been on the run for four months. He told the couple to call him Jim so they did. They did not turn around to see his face.

Twice the car stopped and the gunman ordered Gregsten out to buy cigarettes on one occasion and to fill up with petrol on the other. Gregsten could have made a run for it. There were people around. Why didn't he raise the alarm? His lover was still in the car and presumably Gregsten feared that if he did anything like that then the gunman would kill Valerie.

The couple spent six terrifying hours in the company of the gunman. He spoke in a Cockney accent – the accent of working class Londoners. On a number of occasions he said "be quiet will you I am thinking." He pronounced the 'th' like an 'f' which is a feature of the Cockney accent.

Finally the kidnapper had them park in a layby on the A6. The location was named Deadman's Hill. It was in the early hours of the morning. He tried to tie Valerie up and managed to do so. He asked Gregsten for the bag full of clothes which was at Gregsten's feet. Gregsten leaned forward to get it and when he went to pass it over, the gunman shot him twice in the head.

The woman shrieked and swore at the gunman. He claimed that Gregsten had scared him by moving too fast.

Later he raped Miss Storie. As he was having intercourse with her a car drove by. The headlights illuminated the interior of the Morris Minor for a few seconds. She got a good look at her rapist's face. He then permitted her to dress. The mysterious man ordered her to show him how to drive the car – where the lights were and so on. She was ordered out of the car and onto the road. He then fired seven bullets at her. Five hit her. She fell and played dead.

The man drove off with the gears screaming. He clearly had very little experience with cars. The Morris Minor was seen being driven erratically. In 1961 very few people had cars. Two men in another vehicle were overtaken by the Morris Minor. They drove to catch up with it and got a good look at its occupant.

At 6 am on 23rd August, Miss Storie was found by an undergraduate doing a traffic survey. She immediately said she had been shot and so had the man. Was the man lying there dead, the undergraduate inquired. Valerie believed he was dead. The undergraduate felt for a pulse. Before he could gauge whether Gregsten had a pulse he instantly noticed that the body was stone cold. Gregsten was as dead as a doornail. He had been shot over three hours earlier.

He spoke to her as he waited for help. He noted down all the particulars on pieces of paper he had taken for the purpose of his traffic survey. The student was writing down all the testimony because he recognised that there was a high chance that Valerie would die from her injuries before the ambulance arrived. The police later arrived and the notes were handed over to them. The undergraduate never saw the notes again. Valerie said that the killer and rapist was about thirty years old.

The Morris Minor was found the next day in Redbridge. The car had been wiped clean of finger prints. The crime had been carried out in a very haphazard manner. However, the way that the criminal dealt with the car was crafty. It would probably take a seasoned criminal to do this.

There was a media storm. The case shocked the United Kingdom. There was wall to wall coverage in the newspapers on the radio and on television. The case became known as the A6 murder.

Did the gunman want money and the car? The couple had repeatedly offered him that. Why did he spend six hours with them? Why did he kill Gregsten? There was no particular reason to do so. Perhaps the gunman's explanation was true. He just panicked and shot Gregsten thinking he was reaching for a weapon in the bag or something. Or was it genuinely unintentional – touching the trigger accidentally? Why did the kidnapper reveal so much about himself? Was it always his intention to kill the couple? Or did he only make up his mind much later? What was the gunman doing in that field? The field was not near a railway station and a couple of miles from a bus stop. Did he walk there, or cycle there or drive there? Perhaps someone gave him a lift. Maybe he was trying to burgle houses and was then at a loss for a means of transport. Perhaps the car hijacking was opportunistic. He needed to get out of the area saw a car and that was that. It was very unwise of the kidnapper to say so much about himself. Having done that did he then decide that he had to kill the pair so that he could not be traced? Some days later spent cartridges were found in a basement room in the Vienna Hotel London. It was a very down market hotel. The cartridges were proven by ballistics tests to have come from the murder weapon. The manager had been suspicious of a young man who had not emerged for days. The man in question was Peter Louis Alphon who had been in the same pub as the couple the night of the murder.

A gun, wrapped in a handkerchief, was found hidden under the back seat of the 36A bus in London. There were sixty rounds of ammunition with it. The police put out a statement saying that they suspected Alphon in this case. Alphon handed himself in to the police. It was midnight when he did so. The senior policeman in the case, Acott, came straight away. Acott interviewed Peter Alphon for five hours in the middle of the night.

The following day Miss Storie came to an identity parade. Alphon was there along with several other men of about the same description.

She identified a volunteer as the rapist and not Alphon. The police questioned Alphon ferociously. In those days they would be openly hostile and scathing. They would do everything they could to intimidate someone without physically harming him. In some cases they did physically harm suspects. Alphon stood up to the harsh interrogation. He was an experienced criminal and knew how to handle police interviews. He was not easily intimidated. He said he spent the night of the murder with his mother before going to the Alexandra Court Hotel. Mrs Alphon did not exactly confirm it. She said she had seen her son on that night or possibly the night before or after. She could not remember the exact date. The police had no fingerprints, no positive ID and no confession. Alphon was released. By handing himself in to the police had been in his favour. He refused to give samples of his body fluids or to reveal where the clothes were that he had worn on the day of the murder. He would not disclose where his luggage was. He may have believed that forensics would tie him to the murder. But why then hand himself in?

He had registered at the Alexandra Court Hotel as Frederick Durrant. Why use a pseudonym? He may have been trying to conceal his whereabouts. On the other hand it did not help him establish an alibi.

Another person had stayed in the Vienna Hotel. He had signed in as J Ryan.

A hotel employee William Nudds was unsure who had stayed in the basement room. Was it J Ryan or was it Alphon? Nudds contradicted himself on this. He recalled that J Ryan asked directions to the 36 bus. The gun was found on bus 36 A. Not bus 36. But was it the hotel owner getting it slightly wrong? Or was it J Ryan getting it slightly wrong? Nudds was a petty criminal and had been a police informer. The police suspected that Nudds was changing his story in a way that he thought would ingratiate him with the police. They told him as much. William Nudds then confirmed that he was saying whatever he assumed the police wanted him to say to help them build their case.

There is a tendency to prefer letters that one finds in one's own name. The letters 'R Y A and N' all appear in Hanratty. Ryan is also an Irish surname like Hanratty. James Hanratty was a man of subnormal intelligence. The name Ryan is so short that even he could spell it. Hanratty's initial was 'J'. The gunman had told the couple to call him 'Jim' which is a nickname for anyone called 'James.' Hanratty was known as 'Jimmy' to his family. That is interchangeable with 'Jim'. Would Hanratty have been stupid enough to tell his kidnap victims his real name? Maybe he would. That is especially so if he intended to kill them. If he had planned to kill Michael Gregsten and Valerie Storie all along then it would not matter if he divulged his familiar name 'Jim'.

The English police received a phone call from Ireland. A man with a bed and breakfast had had a young Englishman stay with him some time before. The guest signed in as J Ryan. He said he was bad at writing and asked the guest house owner to write a postcard for him. J Ryan dictated for the other man to write. J Ryan's mother was 'Mrs Hanratty.'

The police then published statements in a newspaper saying they wished to speak to James Hanratty in relation to the A6 murder. James Hanratty called the police several times to say he was not involved in the A6 murder. Why would he do this? Perhaps he was doing so because the police were implying he was the killer.

The police were getting anxious. It was embarrassing. They came under intense public pressure to produce results. Since the day she was found Miss Storie had asked the police to guarantee that her rapist would be brought to justice.

On September 7th a man broke into a house in Richmond-upon-Thames, London and assaulted a woman. He bragged that he was the A6 killer. The woman picked out this man at an identity parade. It was Peter Alphon. But the police had already excluded him as a suspect. They were very closed minded on this.

HANRATTY - THE FINAL CURTAIN

In October James Hanratty was arrested in Blackpool. The police were legally entitled to take his fingerprints even without his permission. The police already had his fingerprints because he had been arrested several times. He volunteered to give hair, blood and saliva samples. He was not legally required to do so. Presumably he thought this would exonerate him. But he was a man of very limited logic ability. So he might have given these samples even if they would have been damning. It turned out that Hanratty has the same blood group as the killer. But 50% of the UK population have that same blood group.

He agreed that the police could take hair, blood and saliva samples from him. He also allowed them to take fibre from his clothes. He was not legally obliged to do this. Some have said this militates towards him being innocent. On the other hand he may have been so dim that he did not understand the significance of what he was agreeing to. Alphon, on the other hand, had refused to do so. Does this suggest guilt? No, because Alphon could have thought that the police would use these items to fit him up – to plant evidence. Moreover, there would have been other crimes that Alphon committed and these samples could have tied him to them.

Hanratty had bright red hair. He felt this made him conspicuous. He dyed it black. He did a very bad job of it. Valerie said her assailant had fair hair. Could this have been her description of red hair badly dyed black? Bear in mind that she only saw him in the light for a few seconds when another car drove by. This lit up the interior of the Morris Minor for a few seconds. In this situation the inside of the car would not have been properly illuminated. In such a situation the colours would not appear properly.

Before the identity parade Hanratty allegedly said to one of the volunteers that he had committed the crime but was cocksure he would get away with it. This statement comes from the volunteer.

Acott came up from London to interview Hanratty. The police made interview notes. The suspect was interviewed without the presence of a lawyer. This was typical for the time. Moreover, the interview notes are since proven to have been falsified. The interview notes were written up. They were later rewritten. There were well over twelve thousand files on the case that the police had. Much of this was never shown to the defence.

In one of the interviews Hanratty allegedly said, "I want to kip". "Kip" is British slang for "sleep". This was a phrase that the gunman had used twice according to Valerie Storie. The police officer had Hanratty uttering this phrase at 9:30 in the morning. Some have taken this as a blatant fabrication on the part of an officer of the law. The aim being to establish that the expression "I want to kip" was typical of Hanratty and therefore he was the killer. Even if he had said it the phrase was not uncommon.

It is more than possible that he would have been sleepy at 9:30 am especially if he had been awake for many hours. The stress of being suspected of murder might have given him a sleepless night. He might have been asking to slumber because the interview was going badly and he feared being incriminated.

There was an identity parade. Hanratty was the only one with reddish hair. The police felt this was unfair. They wondered if they should make all the participants wear hats. In the end the police did not make anyone wear a hat. Miss Storie came in. She took up to 15 minutes to make an identification. Before she did so she had them all speak. She picked out Hanratty. Why did she take so long to pick him out?

Does that undermine her identification? Or did she just want to be certain? She had got it wrong at the Alphon ID parade. Two men had seen the driver of the Morris Minor. One picked out Hanratty. The other said it was not Hanratty. The man who had caught a glimpse of the driver of the Morris Minor had only seen the man for a few seconds from the side. Moreover, it might have been a different Morris Minor.

James Hanratty was charged with murder. Strangely he was not charged with attempted murder, rape, kidnapping and car theft. Mr Hanratty had a friend called Mr France who said that Hanratty found the 36A bus to be a good place to hide stolen goods. He did not say that Hanratty had hidden guns there.

The killer had said, "I have been on the run for four months." Hanratty had been released from prison five months before the killing. If the killer was Hanratty then Hanratty had got this detail wrong. But four months or five months is almost the same. It depends how precise one is. What if it was more like four and a half months? Or did Valerie forget what he said? The words "for five months" could easily be confused with "for four months." Some say that there was a bid to frame

Hanratty. If so could this have been part of it?

The killer appeared to be a dreadful driver. Whatever Hanratty's other limitations he was an accomplished driver. Would he have ground his gears and not known where the lights were? In the stress of the moment he might have panicked and forgotten the basics. As his adrenaline was pumping he might have made some fundamental errors like that. Perhaps he had never driven a Morris Minor.

The prosecution claimed that Hanratty deliberately drove badly to make it appear that it was not him. That beggars belief. Of all the blinds to conceal his identity that is the most improbable. Moreover, the killer clearly assumed that Valerie Storie was dead. There was no need to drive badly on purpose.

There were eight witnesses who swore that they saw Hanratty in Liverpool the day before the murder. That was a Monday.

Gregsten had a logbook in his car. He recorded his journeys in pedantic detail. The police came into possession of the logbook. Acott used the mileometer to calculate that after the murder the car was driven 200 miles. That is much longer than directly from Deadman's Hill to Redbridge. Therefore the route of the car from Deadman's Hill to Redbridge was circuitous and no one knows what route was taken. Those who identified Hanratty as the driver of the Morris Minor may well have seen a different Morris Minor. Indeed those who said that the driver of the Morris Minor was not Hanratty might also have seen the wrong Morris Minor. However, the killer drove the car about 3 o'clock on a weekday morning so there will have been very, very few cars on the road. The chances of someone seeing another Morris Minor on the same route at about the right time are very low indeed.

Two men claimed to have seen Hanratty driving the car through Ilford at 7 am. As the car was driven two hundred miles from Deadman's Hill to Redbridge it went a very roundabout route and would very probably not have been passing through Ilford at 7 am. It went into Avonmore Crescent. The Morris Minor seen at Ilford, near Redbridge, at that time could have been any Morris Minor. The witnesses did not claim to have remembered its registration number. The information about the car driving over two hundred miles from Deadman's Hill to Redbridge was not revealed to the defence. This would have been very useful to the defence. Then again the men who saw a grey Morris Minor who stated that the driver was not Hanratty could have seen the wrong Morris Minor. Wilfully withholding helpful information from the defence is prosecutorial misconduct.

Consider the erratic conduct of the kidnapper. Sitting in the car with his hostages for two hours whilst it was stationary was purposeless. If he wanted to rob or rape or murder he could have done these things. Holding people hostage was to no avail.

Then he had Michael Gregsten drive on a wild goose chase around London and the Home Counties. The gunman had no idea where he wanted to go. He was changeable and aimless. After the murder the gunman drove two hundred miles and ended up less than 50 miles distant from the site of the murder. This yet again shows purposelessness. Was it that he could not read the road signs? Hanratty was illiterate so this might explain it. James Hanratty was a not very successful thief.

Changing his alibi seems to fit the pattern.

On the other hand Alphon had no difficulty reading the signs. He wished to avoid conviction but handed himself in. Once eliminated from inquiries he went to the trial rather than distance himself from proceedings. Only three months after the death of Hanratty people were astonished that Alphon began to hint that he, not Hanratty, was the killer. His admission to the murder and then retraction and then admission and then retraction might suggest that he was the sort of man who would be as irrational and as fickle as the kidnapper.

While Hanratty was awaiting trial another remand prisoner said that Hanratty had confessed to him that he had killed Gregsten. The police subsequently spoke at the stoolpigeon's trial and asked the court to go easy on him because he had assisted the police.

Hanratty was born into a working class family. He left school at fifteen and did some dead end jobs. He soon became a criminal. He was a pathological liar and was diagnosed as psychopathic. If Hanratty was suspected of murder today he might be judged too mentally ill to stand trial. Alternatively, he might be held to be mentally a child.

Initially the case was to be heard at the Old Bailey. Then it was decided that it would be held at Bedford – near the scene of the crime. Some feared local prejudice. As the crime had taken place there the jury might feel duty bound to convict.

Peter Alphon went to hear the trial. Strangely, the jury was not told that Mr Gregsten had been having an affair with Miss Storie at the time of the murder.

Could that extra-marital affair have provided an explanation for an otherwise motiveless murder? If the jurors had been informed that Miss Storie was having an extramarital relationship with Mr Gregsten then that might have made them less likely to believe her.

The defence's story was that James Hanratty had been in Liverpool on the day of the murder. He was with three friends but refused to identify them. His life was on the line but he refused to name them. Not very convincing is it? Perhaps they were fellow criminals and identifying them might have linked them to crimes committed in that city on that day.

James Hanratty mentioned two people he spoke to in Liverpool – shop assistants.

Two of them remembered him. But they could not be sure they met him on 22nd August. Clearly the defendant had been in Liverpool at some point. But the date in question was not necessarily that time. He was arrested in Blackpool in October – not far from Liverpool. It is possible that he passed through Liverpool between the date of the A6 killing and the day of his arrest. Liverpool is a port city on the Irish Sea and many ferries sail from there to Ireland. Hanratty had reason to pass through Liverpool because he sailed to and from Ireland on many occasions.

He changed his alibi from being in Liverpool on the day of the murder to being in Rhyl. However, there is evidence that he was in London the day of the murder. He picked up his dry cleaning in London that day and was at someone's house at 4 pm. If he was in London on the day of the kidnapping then this weakens his claim to have been in Liverpool or Rhyl. Being in London on the day of the abduction would have placed him near the scene of the crime.

The killer did not approach the car until 9:30pm. There is no evidence that Hanratty was near Maidenhead that evening. It is very easy to get from London to Maidenhead in five and a half hours.

Mr Michael Sherrard was the defence barrister of James Hanratty. He tried to convince his client not to change his alibi. Mr Hanratty would not hear of it. Sherrard, counsel for the defence, insisted that his client would be shooting himself in the foot if he did so. But Hanratty was adamant. His brief asked him to sign a statement to the effect that he had been advised that changing his story would fatally undermine his defence. He did so. Cognizant of the terminal effect that altering his alibi might have on him he did so nonetheless.

Miss Storie's spine had been hit by a bullet which left her paralyzed for life.

In the witness box James Hanratty came over as overbearing and sneering. His hostile and haughty demeanour did not produce a congenial impression on the jury. As a hardened criminal his arrogance was to be expected. On the other hand Valerie Storie was tranquil, composed and unwavering. Her quiet dignity won the hearts of the jurors. Mr Sherrard prefaced his cross examination by stating that everyone had the deepest empathy for her monstrous ordeal and no one diminished the horror of that one iota. An innocent man had already been killed in this sordid affair. Sherrard did not want to see a second innocent man killed. There is no question which of Hanratty and Miss Storie was more likeable. The case came down to which of them the jury preferred to believe. Valerie Storie was the Crown's star witness. Her identification was the key plank of the prosecution's case.

The fact that Miss Storie was engaged in an adulterous relationship with Gregsten was not mentioned to the jury. Given the customs of this time this would have damaged her image. There might even have been some who, learning of the adultery would have thought that the couple got what they deserved. The affair was not strictly relevant to the case.

Witnesses swore that Hanratty was in Liverpool on the day of the murder. Some swore that he was in Rhyl. Hanratty had perjured himself with one of his alibis. But which one? Or was it both? His credibility was destroyed.

The jury retired to consider the verdict. After several hours they asked for a definition of beyond reasonable doubt. The judge gave them guidance. Then they returned with a verdict.

Hanratty was found guilty. The judge asked the defendant if he had anything to say. He repeated his denial. The judge then donned the black cap and pronounced the sentence of death.

There was an appeal. It was dismissed by the House of Lords which then functioned as the Supreme Court. There was a campaign for a reprieve. The Home Secretary could advise Her Majesty the Queen to exercise the royal prerogative of mercy. The Queen always went by the advice of her ministers. She had the legal power to commute a death sentence to life imprisonment. The Home Secretary decided that there was no case for a reprieve.

Charles France was a friend of Hanratty's who testified against him. After James Hanratty's appeal failed Mr France committed suicide. France left a suicide note stating that he felt terrible for the suffering he had caused the Hanratty family. Perhaps the family should have tried to internationalise the case. James Hanratty was born in England to Irish parents. The child of an Irish parent has the right to Irish citizenship. The Hanratty family could have asked the Irish Government to intervene. The idea that an innocent Irishman was due to be hanged in England would have incensed Ireland. The huge protests might have convinced the Home Secretary to recommend that the royal prerogative of mercy be exercised. Then the Queen would have been graciously pleased to commute the sentence to life imprisonment.

The night before Mr Hanratty was due to be put to death he told his father he would "take it like a man." In fairness to James Hanratty the only account of the execution states that he did indeed demonstrate unutterable courage.

He maintained his innocence to the end. On 4th April he was hanged. There were no complications. A witness to his death recalled that the he "strutted" in and maintained his defiant composure to the very end.

After the execution of Hanratty, a gay couple befriended Peter Alphon. One of these men was named Jean Justice, the son of a Belgian diplomat, became fixated with the case.

The gay couple wined and dined Alphon. He told them on numerous occasions that he was the A6 killer. Was this him talking nonsense when drunk? Was he telling them what they wanted to hear? He was singing for his supper. On the other hand it may have been a case of *in vino veritas*. A drunken man speaks the truth.

They recorded Alphon on the phone without his knowledge. They had recordings of him making incriminating statements. When he discovered that he had been recorded without his permission he flew into a rage. He also told them that he had received five thousand pounds from a man for ending the affair between Mr Gregsten and Miss Storie. Who was this man? Alphon had no job and deposited seven thousand six hundred pounds into his account between October 1961 and June 1962. That was a phenomenal amount of money for the time. October 1961 was the month that Hanratty was charged with murder. Note that Alphon did not say he was paid to kill – only to end the affair. Who would want the affair ended?

The blatant suspect would be Mrs Gregsten. But she seemed to have accepted the split from her husband. Miss Storie said her affair was no explanation for the murder. Mrs Gregsten visited her in hospital and the two got on well. Moreover, five thousand pounds was a staggering sum at the time. It was like one hundred and thirty thousand pounds today. Mrs Gregsten was a housewife and her husband was a government scientist. They did not have that kind of money. The claim of receiving five thousand pounds to end the affair is likely to be bogus. That does not disprove Alphon's unpressured confession to the murder.

Where did the the seven thousand five hundred pounds deposited in Alphon's account come from? Presumably he was a very successful thief. Or did Justice and Fox pay him some money?

Mr Alphon appeared to feel guilt-stricken about the death of Hanratty. He visited the Hanratty family and commiserated with them. It is surely surprising that they allowed him into their house. If Hanratty had not killed Gregsten then who had? The obvious other suspect is Alphon. If Alphon had confessed at the time then Hanratty would not have been hanged. Tellingly, Mr Alphon did not seem to feel a twinge of sympathy for Mr Gregsten or Miss Storie.

In 1967 Alphon took the extraordinary step of calling a press conference in Paris.

He announced that he murdered Gregsten. He had put himself in legal jeopardy. A posthumous appeal could be allowed – clearing Hanratty. People were zealously campaigning for this at the time. John Lennon walked around with a sign saying 'Britain murdered Hanratty'. In 1949 Timothy Evans was hanged for murder. In 1952 his conviction was posthumously overturned. John Christie was convicted for those murders for which Evans had previously been wrongly convicted. Christie was then executed. So in 1967 Alphon could have been talking his way to the gallows. That year he went on ITN to say that he carried out the A6 murder. John Lennon financed a documentary about the A6 case. It was fronted by Paul Foot. The veteran ultra-left journalist argued that Hanratty was innocent of the crime.

Alphon wrote a lengthy confession which he gave to Jean Justice. Mr Justice published a book entitled 'Murder is Murder' in France. Justice gave these to the Home Office. It outlined the case against Alphon. Alphon said that he decided to kill the couple because of the sort of people they were. Was this because they were adulterers? Or because they were of a certain social class? He said that he had given Mr Gregsten two chances to escape but Gregsten had failed to do so. This was probably an allusion to the opportunity to run away at the petrol station and the shop. Some have taken this as proof positive of Alphon's guilt as he could not have known about the two occasions in which Gregsten was allowed out of the car by the kidnapper. However,

Alphon could easily have known about the particulars of the kidnapping without being the killer. The police may have told him about this when they questioned him. Moreover, the newspapers detailed the ordeal. Lastly during the trial, Miss Storie gave a full account of the event.

Mr Alphon stated in 1966 that his taped confession and written confession was him inventing a work of fiction. He was helping Jean Justice write a novel. If Justice really thought that he was a killer was it not unwise to hang around with him? This was especially so if Alphon committed the murder as part of a crusade against indecency as Alphon said. Homosexuality was legally termed indecency at the time. The death penalty was suspended in 1965. It was not abolished. There was much talk about ending the suspension. Hanging could easily have been reintroduced. In fact in 1970 it was abolished. Even then Alphon would have faced a life sentence. Is it crazier to confess if you are guilty or innocent?

The behaviour of the kidnapper fits with Alphon's personality. He was very boastful and unstable. That is why he was rabbiting on to the couple in the car. Another fact that points towards Alphon being guilty is that Hanratty spoke hesitantly and left very long pauses in his speech. Alphon's conversational patter was of a reasonable speed. It was not like a machine gun. The killer spoke with a Cockney accent which Alphon did not. Instead Alphon spoke Standard British English but when he was stressed he lapsed into Cockney. The killer's behaviour suggests grave anxiety. Alphon did not know how to drive. Valerie's evidence suggested that the killer was terrible at driving as did the two other men who had seen the Morris Minor.

Valerie Storie said that it was clear that 'Jim' was not the true name of her rapist. If she is right then this suggests that James Hanratty was innocent. Alphon was the son of a highly ranking Scotland Yard detective. Was Scotland Yard trying to protect its own? His face was more similar to Valerie Storie's identikit description than Hanratty's face. Some think that the police closed ranks to save Alphon. But the police tried to get evidence to convict him. This theory is flawed. As Mr Alphon was in the pub the same time as Gregsten and Miss Storie he could have followed the couple to their car. As he was on foot it would have taken him about forty minutes to get there. Indeed finding it in the dark may have been difficult. Did he go to the Dorney Reach area with the intention of killing the couple? Alternatively it could have been an opportunistic crime. On ITN in 1967 he stated that he killed them as part of a crusade against immorality. He was incensed at their adultery. But if, against expectation, he intended to kill them why did he not shoot them right away? He might have thought he was too close to houses – his shots would be heard. He had been seen in the same pub as them earlier. Perhaps he wanted to get them to a remote location for the killing to take place. Moreover, he might have been steeling himself to go through with it. Could he bring himself to kill? If his actuation was to penalise adultery committing rape was a strange way of expressing strong disapproval.

For years the Hanratty family demanded that the case be reopened. In 1999 they finally got their way. They wanted DNA to be used to have their relative's conviction found unsafe. They said that this would be like winning the lottery.

In 2002 DNA tests proved that the killer was Hanratty. But could his DNA have gotten on the handkerchief in which the gun was kept some other way? Could his DNA have gotten into Valerie's knickers by some other means? The exhibits at the trial often touched each other. There were well over a hundred exhibits. These items were carried together in the same box.

However, how come there is no DNA from Alphon there or Michael Gregsten?

Without the DNA, which was not available in 1962, then the jury should have declared him not guilty.

EPILOGUE

Valerie Storie remained in a wheelchair until her death on 26th March 2016. She was 77 years old.

Peter Alphon died in January 2009 after a fall at his home.

Janet Gregsten died on 25th January 2005.

Is this the Final Curtain for James Hanratty now there is DNA evidence to prove he was guilty or could there be a strong possibility that cross contamination occurred or another government cover up?

The End

Don't miss out!

Visit the website below and you can sign up to receive emails whenever David J Cooper publishes a new book. There's no charge and no obligation.

https://books2read.com/r/B-A-CBBF-AJHSB

BOOKS 2 READ

Connecting independent readers to independent writers.

Did you love *Hanratty - The Final Curtain*? Then you should read *Cold Fury*[1] by David J Cooper!

[2]

A psychopath, a wife's alibi, 3 innocent little girls....

Why would a man, married to an attractive young woman, want to sexually assault and murder innocent little girls?

In the late 1960s, Cannock Chase in Staffordshire became the centre of the biggest murder hunt in Britain.

The bodies of five year old Diane Tift, six year old Margaret Reynolds, and seven year old Christine Darby were found dumped there.

The killer thought he was cleverer than the police and slipped through the net four times.

---

1. https://books2read.com/u/b68VeM

2. https://books2read.com/u/b68VeM

He would have continued with the killings but he made a big mistake.

Find out what happened and how the police eventually caught up with him.

Read more at davidjcooperauthorblog.wordpress.com.

Also by David J Cooper

Penny Lane, Paranormal Investigator
The Witch Board
The House of Dolls
The Devil's Coins
The Mirror
The Key
The Reveal

Standalone
The Devil Knows
The Party's Over
Encuentro Mortal
Se Acabo La Fiesta
Cold Fury
Deadly Encounter
House on the Hill
Hanratty - The Final Curtain

Watch for more at davidjcooperauthorblog.wordpress.com.

About the Author

David J Cooper is a British author. He was born in Darlaston, West Midlands, to a working class family. After leaving school he had jobs ranging from engineering to teaching. He got involved in local politics and became a local councillor in 1980.

His novels incorporate elements of the paranormal, horror, suspense, and mystery.

He is featured in the Best Poems and Poets of 2012 with his first and only poem God's Garden.

He currently lives in a small town in Mexico with his three dogs, Chula, Sooty, and Benji.

Read more at davidjcooperauthorblog.wordpress.com.

Printed in Great Britain
by Amazon

76346714R00068